Practical Psychology 101

A psychological manual for Black Lives Matter and all other movements

Jeff Menzise, Ph.D.

Foreword by:

Camara Jules P. Harrell, Ph.D.

The Manichean Psychology

Practical

Psychology 101:

A
psychological manual
for
Black Lives Matter
and
all other movements

Jeff Menzise, Ph.D.

Foreword by:

Camara Jules P. Harrell, Ph.D.

The Manichean Psychology

Practical Psychology 101: A psychological manual for Black Lives Matter and all other movements.
Copyright ©2017 by Jeff Menzise. All rights reserved. Printed in the United States of America. No part of this book may be used or reproduced in any manner without written permission from the author except in the case of brief quotations embodied in critical articles and reviews. For information address Mind on the Matter Publishing, Post Office Box 755, College Park, Maryland 20741.

10 9 8 7 6 5 4 3 2 1

Cover Design by Jeffery Menzise, Ph.D. for Mind on the Matter Publishing

Library of Congress Cataloging-in-Publication Data
Menzise, Jeffery,
        Practical Psychology 101: A psychological manual for Black Lives Matter and all other movements/ by Jeff Menzise, Ph.D.
includes Foreword, Cover Artwork, & Design

ISBN 978-0-9856657-3-9

Published in 2017 by
Mind on the Matter Publishing,
PO BOX 755, College Park, MD 20741
Website: www.mindonthematter.com
Email: drjeff@mindonthematter.com
Twitter: @drjeffmenzise
Office Phone: 240-988-9639

Dedication

This manual is dedicated to all great organizers and those who have fought and continue to fight for social justice, equality, and freedom. For those who have sacrificed in order that others may someday have the lived experience of their own greatness. For all of my teachers that have ever taught me anything to do with TRUTH, especially those who have lived according to their own words. For those students who will read this manual, I pray that your interest and understanding of the field of psychology is greatly increased and that you will incorporate this knowledge into all that you do.

Acknowledgments

I'd like to acknowledge the people who continually participate, organize, and lead modern movements for social justice. Over the years, I have observed from the frontlines, as well as from afar, the need for psychological training for those who are involved, on all levels. I was inspired to pen this brief manual, as I found myself talking back to the reporters, reports, and pundits on the news, and as I spoke with groups and individuals about the many uprisings that have taken place around the world in the last decade. Based on this, I see that the need is great, and hereby offer you one of my many contributions toward our continued fight for justice.

"The whole of the common characteristics with which heredity endows the individuals of a race constitute the genius of the race. When, however, a certain number of these individuals are gathered together in a crowd for purposes of action, observation proves that, from the mere fact of their being assembled, there result certain new psychological characteristics, which are added to the racial characteristics and differ from them at times to a very considerable degree.

Organized crowds have always played an important part in the life of peoples, but this part has never been of such moment as at present. The substitution of the unconscious action of crowds for the conscious activity of individuals is one of the principal characteristics of the present age." - **Gustav Le Bon - The Crowd: A study of the popular mind** (1896)

"We have still much to learn as to the laws according to which the mind and body act on one another, and according to which one mind acts on another; but it is certain that a great part of this mutual action can be reduced to general laws, and that the more we know of such laws, the greater our power to benefit others will be.

If, when, through the operation of such laws surprising events take place, (and) we cry out..."Such is the will of God," instead of setting ourselves to inquire whether it was the will of God to give us power to bring about or prevent these results; then our conduct is not piety but sinful laziness." - **George Salmon, D.D. - A Sermon on the Work of the Holy Spirit, in Battle for the Mind: A physiology of conversion and brain-washing. by William Sargant (1957)**

Practical Psychology 101: A Psychological Manual for Black Lives Matter

and

All Other Movements

vii

Practical Psychology 101

Foreword

Gradually, like the coming of a new day, I realized that the wheelchair-bound woman I see each morning at the Metro stop was not waiting for the next bus. Sheltered on three sides by plexiglass and iron, this distant daughter of Africa has secured a fixed address: the corner of Georgia and Florida Avenues, Northwest, Washington, D. C. On most days she refuses eye contact. She asks nothing of passers-by or of those who were using the stop for its intended purpose. One of her legs is missing, perhaps a casualty of a battle with Type-2 diabetes. As the days get colder and the nights longer, she huddles beneath thick blankets that have materialized maybe out of thin air. A bus stop is a cruel and undignified home in the spring and summer. It becomes a lethal abode as late autumn surrenders to winter.

In the United States, in a good year, the richest individuals may accumulate wealth at a rate of one million dollars an hour.[1] On streets that are a brief car ride's distance from the homes of the very wealthy, we parade indifferently past the homeless, who cling desperately to the remnants of life. How much of our humanity is stripped away as we stroll by the discarded and dispossessed? What do we become as we strive for the poor prizes that wealth brings and look on the shelter-less like they are no more than fallen leaves?

Too many citizens for too many years have made

---

1   http://www.businessinsider.com/what-warren-buffett-makes-per-hour-2013-12

homes in the alleys and on the grates of American cities. When Dr. Jeff Menzise was finishing his doctoral studies in clinical psychology at Howard University, another woman, tall, Black, and straight had taken up residency on a steam-producing grate next to the Howard University School of Dentistry. She suffered the terrors of mental illness silently, most of the time. On rare occasions, her words emerged as inscrutable salads. One day, perhaps because of the weather or some undignified act in which she engaged, I mentioned her plight to Dr. Menzise. Without a hint of hesitation, he said quietly but firmly that "the sister is a soldier." These five words captured the status and context of this woman's life. Among America's longest war is the one it wages against African people. Casualties on the frontlines rarely make for pleasant viewing. I was certain from the moment Dr. Menzise uttered these words, that his graduation would signal the arrival of a clinical psychologist who would be called anything but ordinary.

Clinical psychologists diagnose and treat mental disorders drawing on all that is learned within the disciplines of general psychology and the neurosciences. We learn best when we teach, and for years Dr. Menzise inspired students in the general psychology courses he taught at Howard University. The broad-based knowledge of psychology reflected in the pages of this book are in part, an outgrowth of Dr. Menzise's clinical training and his years of nurturing developing minds as a teacher.

Basic psychology courses cover topics spanning the biological aspects of behavior, to theory and research in learning, memory, emotions, and personality psychology. Students of African descent can find important principles related to the causes and consequences of behavior in each topic covered in general psychology classes. Many who teach these courses will wish they had written the pages you are about to read. Dr. Menzise shows students how to

Foreword

shape psychological principles into tools for conceptualizing and countering the forces of post-modern racist oppression. He challenges the reader to journey beyond the required mastery of the principles of general psychology. This book invites us to broaden our perspectives and explore the many ways psychological knowledge can be used to relieve human misery and inequities.

But something much larger shapes Dr. Menzise's thinking. He possesses a unique capacity to frame the context, breadth, and status of the actions of people of African descent. Whether we reside on grates or in mansions, he provides an accurate assessment of our circumstances and behaviors. The power of his analysis stems from the broad stance he takes toward his intellectual efforts. Dr. Menzise travels the world in pursuit of truth; no traditional Western paradigm satisfies his curiosity. He incorporates information as old as the knowledge systems of Kemet and as recent as breakthroughs taking place in modern cultural and Africana Studies. His perspective extends far beyond the curricula that he mastered on the way to obtaining his many degrees, certifications, and licenses.

Radically changing one's view of the world is an essential first step toward developing a revolutionary consciousness. Rooting out oppression's structural causes requires us to reshape the cognitive schemata through which we grasp the world. Often, this entails changing our perspective on those who profit from oppression and those who are trampled under its feet. In the new schema, collaborators, be they corporate moguls, thugs, or politicians are no longer glorified. The "wretched of the earth," including those who make their homes at bus stops are conceptualized as our wounded warriors. Dr. Menzise's writings facilitate this kind of change in our mental frameworks.

During the latter years of the last century, Dr.

Practical Psychology 101

Bobby E. Wright operated a mental health center in Chicago, mentored young people, and fashioned sharp critiques of Western psychology. In 1977, the year after I finished graduate school, I discussed Dr. Wright's work with Dr. Keturah Whitehurst, my supervisor at Virginia State University. With a smile, this wise and courageous woman told me that "Bobby's a gadfly." Over the years, my understanding of her comment has deepened. Nature produces quick and persistent creatures that fly in the face of predators or sleeping prey, stimulating them to alter their behaviors. In this book and in all of his writing, Dr. Menzise extends the important legacy of the gadfly. Those looking for a quick and comforting introduction to psychological principles will not find it here. Others who seek a generative, new, and sometimes needling perspective on psychology will be more than satisfied by the profound insights provided in these pages.

Camara Jules P. Harrell
Department of Psychology
Howard University

Chapter 1
An introduction...

The purpose of this manual is to provide insight into the human factor of social movements. As human beings, we are complex, unique, and oft times unaware of all that we bring to the table: the good, bad, beautiful, ugly and indifferent. It is precisely what we bring to the table that determines our success, and even how we define and conceptualize the idea of success and how to attain it. Becoming more aware of ourselves: who we are, our strengths and weaknesses, our assets and liabilities, our self-concept, our insecurities, our dreams, desires, motivations and goals, will allow us to participate more fully and to determine the route most suited for us to travel towards our predefined goals. From the perspective of movement leadership, having this knowledge of one's self, as well as those being led, allows for the proper assigning of roles, and helps to realistically shape expectations and increases the likelihood of success, while decreasing the element of surprise and avoiding potential pitfalls and dangers.

From the perspective of those joining movements in "non-leadership" roles, this information is equally as powerful, for the exact same reasons as listed for those in leadership roles. The difference is the perspective of how the info is applied. For example, instead of assisting with the assigning of roles, this information will help participants to decide whether or not to accept a role, and to choose movements to become involved with, based on their purpose, identity, skills, strengths, weaknesses, etc. This knowledge will also assist participants to assess and analyze the character of those claiming to be leaders, as well as the disposition of their fellow participants.

In order to address this need, I have chosen to highlight a few very important concepts in psychology. In my more than 20 years of studying psychology, I have come to realize that psychology is perhaps the most important subject that any human being can learn and master. Why do you say that Dr. Menzise? I'm glad you asked. I say this because of all the various subjects in the world, psychology is the one that helps you to best understand humans (our thoughts, behavior, personality, and other characteristics). This knowledge is at the core of ALL other subjects that involve human beings including economics, education, entertainment, labor, law, politics, religion, sex, and war. Humans are also at the core of all STEM (Science, Technology, Engineering, and Mathematics), and Artistic expressions as well (STEAM), bringing these subjects under the purview of psychology.

For those of us who have chosen the practical aspects of psychology (i.e., clinical, counseling, industrial/ organizational, experimental, etc.), we have endeavored to master human beingness to one degree or another (although many have never thought of their chosen paths from this perspective). Our training and practical application of what has been discovered about human behavior, thoughts, motivation, personality, identity, etc., provides a unique and powerful experience of what it means to be human. Our researchers, especially those who have participated in laboratory experiments where environments and humans are directly manipulated in order to produce predictable results, help to determine the most efficient and effective ways of modifying human thoughts and behaviors, for the better and sometimes even for the worse.

An introduction...

From Pavlov's dogs to Skinner's rats, and from Watson's Santa Claus mask to Milgram's authority studies, psychology has demonstrated time and time again that humans are easily manipulated, and that we can learn how to manipulate humans, even by using animals.

The link between psychology and all other aspects of human beingness is easily confirmed by the fact that, no matter what the profession, the brain, the mind, the personality, learning and other dispositions are always, and absolutely, involved. It is for this reason that I say "everybody should study and master psychology to one degree or another." Many of my students, of various majors, will confirm that my mantra is for them to at least minor in, if not double-major with psychology, or in some way, master psychology. Imagine the carpenter who has also mastered his human nature, or the dentist who has cleared his mind of all contradictions and is able to maintain lucidity when solving an issue for their patients. What about the childcare provider who has increased their effectiveness, by freeing their unconsciously stored "issues," alleviating all anxieties? Each of these professionals would surely improve the efficiency and effectiveness of not only their work goals, but their personal lives will likely also benefit.

When working with attorneys and trial lawyers, my typical role is to assist them to be better "psychologists" when performing in front of the jury during their opening arguments, cross-examinations, and their closing statements. I assist them to learn how to read the body language of potential jurors during jury selection, and while working as a case consultant, I help them to read into the personalities and minds of the witnesses, defendants, plaintiffs, jurors, and even the opposing counsel. The attorney becomes a magician and an actor, who must embody a particular perspective while translating and transmitting it to the judge and jury, in order to persuade

15

Practical Psychology 101

them to see things in favor of their client. When working with my "Hollywood" clients, the actors and actresses I have coached into various roles and deals, I assist them to embody the character or role they are playing; literally developing the personality, cognition, memories, and other psychological attributes of their character in order that they may fully embody the person, and present a convincing performance.

Speaking of Hollywood, the entire notion of a *Jedi Mind Trick* is totally based on psychology. Being able to manipulate perception and to shape perspectives is what a *Jedi Mind Trick* is, which is 100% psychology. *Spider*, son of *Anansi the Spider* in the book *Anansi Boys*, is a masterful example of this ability. He had the uncanny gift of creating "illusions" in the minds of those he sought to manipulate. Similarly, marketing firms, whose job is also to get people to do things in favor of their clients, do so by shaping and manipulating perceptions and perspectives. This involves the subtle implanting of thoughts and ideas into their target audience. For example, there has been an increase in the number of actors smoking e-cigarettes in music videos. It is often done in the coolest way possible. This in turn, makes it more appealing to the viewer, which then increases the likelihood that they will eventually want to try it. This occurrence happens in direct relationship to the increase of "anti-smoking" campaigns; in other words, stop smoking cigarettes the traditional way, and begin using vaporizing e-cigarettes.

Social media websites are a psychologist's gold mine. With the proper understanding, someone trained in human behavior can observe an individual's profile, their timeline, comments, and posts and develop a pretty clear picture of their personality, disposition, unconscious issues/traumas, desires, insecurities, relationship patterns, etc. All of these can then be used to manipulate the indi-

An introduction...

vidual and groups of individuals; it's the reason for the boom in the analytics business.[2]

Manipulation is not always a bad thing. In fact, every time a client goes to a therapist, life coach, or counselor, they are seeking to be manipulated; whether to overcome a depressed mood, anxiety, compulsive and/or addictive behaviors, or simply to sort through confusing thoughts and patterns of thinking. As practical psychologists, this is one of the four main goals of the discipline, which are: 1) to observe human behavior; 2) to understand human behavior; 3) to predict human behavior; and 4) to manipulate human behavior. In order to achieve these goals, we must figure out all the components that eventually lead to, and that comprise human behaviors.

The wise ones will see that these four goals are most beneficial when first applied to themselves; the fool will immediately try to figure out how they can apply it to others in an attempt to gain some sort of advantage and control. The latter attitude is usually a sure sign of insecurity, especially when there is a strong "need" to be in control, motivating such a position.

Preachers, people in sales, psychologists, attorneys, journalists, marketing firms, personal trainers, parents, and just about anybody can benefit from the ability to manipulate. For this reason, this manual is designed to assist the serious organizer to observe and better understand themselves, to the point to where they are capable of manipulating their own psychology towards a more healthy and balanced expression, and decrease their susceptibility to being unknowingly, and unwillingly manipulated by others. Ideally, this will increase their efficiency and effectiveness as an organizer and social justice activist.

Stated another way: To become a better leader

---

2   http://www.businessinsider.com/analytics-firm-crimson-hexagon-uses-social-media-to-predict-stock-movements-2017-4

and/or organizer, you want to become the most efficient and effective version of you, that you can possibly be; the best way to do this is to understand and master psychology. This almost guarantees that whatever you involve yourself in, you will perform with an improved focus, a deeper insight, and will more likely be successful (however that is defined) at the task. Imagine an activity that usually makes you anxious, i.e., gives you "butterflies," shaky hands, and/or a feeling of nervousness; now imagine performing that activity minus this emotional experience with an added level of confidence and mental clarity.

Imagine if instead of using your energies to generate and maintain that emotional state, you were able to take that energy and employ it towards a more productive goal like improving your physical health, or passing a major exam. The energy that runs emotions is the same energy that runs everything else; it is simply being guided towards generating a physiological response (hormone release, activation of neurotransmitters, etc.), subsequent physical sensations, and fueling thoughts, that in turn, generate more physical sensations…becoming a sort of emotional feedback loop.

Specific to our subject of psychology, much of what takes place in social activism is predictable, and easy to manipulate. For example, in current times, when unarmed American African men and women seem to be getting shot more frequently by law enforcement officers and vigilante civilians, there has also been an increase of public outrage and open protest. We've seen it in Ferguson and we've seen it in Baltimore. In each case, there was an organized response to the injustice, and there was also a seemingly intentional obstruction of these organized responses to injustice. There were rumors of individuals posing as "protesters," who were actually there to provoke discord and violence. There is evidence that companies are actu-

An introduction...

ally hiring "actors" to pose as protesters and participants at rallies.[3] I have personally spoken with "protesters" who seemed out of place at a "peaceful rally," who were, in fact, on some alternative mission. In one particular situation, their intentions were made obvious to me because I noticed that one of the "protesters" was wearing a bulletproof vest under his t-shirt. I walked over and struck up a simple conversation and eventually asked about his t-shirt and the body armor beneath it. He was surprised by my observation, and even more surprised by my audacity to inquire about it and his reason for being at the "peaceful protest." He claimed to be there working security.

The point in sharing this example is to demonstrate how "consciousness" plays a major part in how we operate on a day-to-day basis; in this case, how it plays out in the form of environmental and situational awareness, while engaged in protests and demonstrations. This is just one of the five areas of psychology covered in this brief manual. The other four are: Emotions, Personality, Identity, and Learning. I will take each of these five areas and give three perspectives: 1) the "typical" Western/modern psychological perspective; 2) an African psychological perspective; and 3) how the subject relates to organizing and community activism. These will be presented sometimes in a very linear and distinguishable manner, and at other times as an interwoven narrative merging all three perspectives at once. There will, however, be very clear statements of how an organizer and/or activist can apply knowledge of each subject in their daily activities throughout each of the related chapters.

It is my hope that this manual will provide insight to those who are called to organize for social justice, both on an individual and group level. My hope is that this in-

---

3   http://www.zerohedge.com/news/2017-08-16/why-was-crowd-hire-company-recruiting-25-hour-political-activists-charlotte-last-wee

Practical Psychology 101

formation will help them to better understand themselves and other people, with whom they are working for and/or against. It is also my hope to pique the interest of my readers in the subject and practical applications of psychology, both as an academic discipline and as a very real aspect of being human. I maintain that it is one of the most important subjects to be explored, regardless of race, class, gender, and location on the planet. By continuing to evolve our understanding of the human mind, we will hopefully continue to evolve the human mind. With this growth and development, perhaps we will one day bring forth peace and justice to all people.

Before we can claim progress we must come to terms with the healing that needs to take place. If we continue to pretend that the injury does not exist, and that there is not a continual assault being launched against us, there can be no progress made towards establishing justice. The harsh reality is that many profit by maintaining the lie, and therefore, they perpetuate the injury and intentional deception. Malcolm X provides a sharp and certain illustration of this in the following quote about progress:

> If you stick a knife in my back 9 inches and pull it out 6 inches, there is no progress. If you pull it all the way out, that's not progress. The progress is healing the wound that the blow made. And they haven't even begun to pull the knife out, much less try to heal the wound. They won't even admit the knife is there.

I challenge you to seek true progress by uncovering that which needs healing, both in your personal life, and that of your community. Establish a plan to not only remove the knife, but to restore a healthy balance to that which has been injured. The work is not easy, but it is fruitful. I wish you luck and divine guidance on your journey.

Chapter 2
Literally, the study of the soul

In modern times, psychology is defined as the scientific study of behavior and mental processes.[4] This science exists for the purpose of explaining, describing, observing, predicting, manipulating and controlling behavior and mental processes. I will seek to elaborate on each of these concepts below, and ask that you keep in mind that each point is directly connected to the next, and that they may occur in various ways, and be undertaken in a non-sequential fashion; meaning you could seek to predict and control behavior, without first trying to explain and describe it, and vice versa.

When it comes to explaining and describing behaviors and mental processes, we are seeking to better understand the "what," "why," and "how" of the observed behaviors. A description is basically a listing of attributes, qualities, and characteristics, while the explanation is an exploration of how and why those attributes and characteristics have come to be, and how they play out in the total dynamic of the topic, including the motivating forces soliciting, propelling and at times compelling them.

Such descriptives and explanations make up the majority of psychological literature, which is full of the-

thinking, memory, perception, emotions, problem solving, etc.

ories proposed by those who have given deep levels of thought and evaluation to the various topics. Researchers in the field, those that actively conduct experiments, as well as those who develop theories, have accumulated a vast record of data, against which new thoughts and ideas are measured, forming a psychological paradigm we call "modern psychology." It is important to understand what is meant by the word "modern" when used as an adjective for academic and professional subjects.

As with all words, there are several definitions, some of which are very similar to others, and some that are totally different. Because psychology is also a highly political field, I like to reference the definition of "modern" relating to a very significant point in European history, the Middle Ages. In this context, "modern" refers specifically to the period of time after the Middle Ages, known as the Renaissance, or literally the "rebirth." It's a time when Europe was recovering from the "Dark Ages" and finally emerging as a collection of civilizations beyond the early Roman empire.

It's important to acknowledge this, especially in academic discourse, because it situates the subject in a period of European recovery; when they were finally able to present themselves as a global power and force that would soon set out to colonize the planet and information about the same. To study pre-modern European psychology would present an entirely different set of values, worldviews, information, concepts, and dispositions than that presented by a study of modern European psychology. Additionally, the term "modern" also situates the study of psychology beyond the ancient concepts of psychology, not only those held by Europeans, but also those created, explored, established, maintained, and expanded by the many non-White civilizations around the world. Keep in mind the fact that these civilizations existed thousands of

Literally, the study of the soul

years prior to the rise and peaking of the Roman Empire. This understanding is valuable especially because it sets the context within which much of psychology is oriented, and will provide a socio-historical and political context as we explore the practical aspects of psychology throughout this manual.

When describing behaviors and mental processes, psychologists create specific categories, and subsequently work to catalogue their findings accordingly. This is what we have in the Diagnostic and Statistical Manual of Mental Disorders (DSM) series. It is literally the detailed explanation and classification of what the APA (American Psychiatric Association) has agreed to label mental disorders and psychopathology. The DSM is complete with diagnostic criteria and features, and how the disorders manifest differently across gender, age, race and culture. The DSM describes the course of mental illness—meaning it describes how pathology progresses from its onset to the advanced stages—and also how to distinguish one disorder from the others with similar characteristics and symptoms. The DSM does a wonderful job of explaining the "what" of mental disorders, and also provides some perspectives regarding the "why."

From another viewpoint, psychological explanations are used to understand concepts such as learning, memory, human development, consciousness, and the many other psychology-based "specialty areas." For example, learning theorists may seek to explain the impact of environmental feedback on the ability of an individual to acquire new knowledge and information (we will see more on this in a later chapter). Developmental psychologists may seek to explain how the developing human being comes to acquire their specific and unique characteristics, regarding both their physical features as well as their cognitive, social, and personality-based dispositions.

Practical Psychology 101

The neuropsychologists among us may seek to explain the relationships between brain structure, brain functioning, neurochemistry, observable behaviors and internal experiences.

While being able to answer the "why" behind experiences, responses, and daily occurrences is perhaps the driving force behind most scientific endeavors, the ability to predict and control the same is probably much more valuable in the world of practical psychology. These ideas can rightly be viewed as different sides of the same coin because of the obvious relationship between them.

The psychologist seeking to predict and control behavior is usually doing so for the purpose of helping individuals, families, couples, communities, societies, and nations, to function in a more productive, adaptable and healthy fashion. Predicting behavior and mental processes allows for the successful anticipation of certain events, responses and reactions, and subsequently, the proper preparation to capitalize on the behaviors and/or thoughts, or to avoid their occurrence altogether. Evidence of the perceived power of predictability, or being able to predict, is seen in the large numbers of people who play games of chance, wherein they have to predict the outcome of a dice roll, a lottery number, a boxing match, or some other major sports event. People have so much faith in the predictable nature of such events that they will literally wager small (or sometimes large) fortunes on their predicted outcome.

In regards to controlling and manipulating human behavior, the entire world of marketing is developed based on this science of predicting how people will respond to commercials, advertisements and various forms of stimulation. Economics is also based on faith in the predictability of human response. The best economists are those who are able to predict with consistent accuracy how people will

Literally, the study of the soul

respond to global happenings, the news and information received, and their emotional ties to certain outcomes.

Psychic readings and life coaches are also measured by their ability to successfully advise their clients on a particular course of action, based on minimal, unseen, or unknown information. The ability to predict how one might benefit, or how one may avoid a catastrophe is why people seek the advice of those with these predictive skills. This has been the case since the most ancient of times, where people sought out their priesthood and various oracles in order to gain insight and guidance around certain issues and life circumstances. Two of the most masterful examples of the use of predictability are found in the ancient Nile Valley civilization of Kemet (Egypt).

The priesthood and scientists were able to predict the flooding and receding of the Nile River using the "Nilometer" found on Elephantine Island (known as "Abu" to the ancients). They were also able to predict and chart the procession of the stars in the heavens as demonstrated by many of their temple structures including the "zodiac" displayed on the ceiling of the Temple of Denderah. These observations and predictions were a major part of building the thriving civilizations that many are currently studying and exploring with pure awe and fascination.

The science of interrogation is also based on the ability to predict and interpret the meaning underlying observable behaviors and speech, banking on the unconscious triggering of actions that can then be interpreted. Micro-facial expressions, unconscious behaviors, bio-feedback, and the study of body language are all examples of usable tools, based on the inherent value of being able to predict and discern the relationship between seemingly unrelated points of data (behaviors and intentions).

When seeking to control behavior, psychologists look to theories of motivation and have constructed theories of learning to reflect what they have found. It is here that we find information about why we do what we do (motivation). In a nutshell, humans and animals tend to seek pleasure and reward, while avoiding punishment and pain;[5] and thus, are capable of being motivated by pleasure, punishment, reward, and pain. Typically, the more subtle and undetectable the attempts to control behavior and thoughts, the more effective and efficient these attempts become. This is because of the human drive towards autonomy, and thus the tendency to resist and avoid overt attempts of being controlled without consent or in spite of their will and desire to decide for themselves, free of coercion.[6]

In psychoanalysis, this is demonstrated by the *ego defense mechanisms* and is avoided by not going directly after the problem, but instead, allowing the client to explore the content of their subconscious minds via *free association*, hopefully discovering the root of their issues for themselves. To achieve this, the skilled analyst steers the conversation, at times unintentionally, towards the problem areas without seeming to do so, and will thus avoid arousing certain aspects of defensiveness within their client, thereby granting access to the subconscious and unconscious material of the mind.

As can be observed by the above statements, psychology is a very powerful science to be mastered. This mastery is measured by the practitioner's knowledge of the human being, and the efficiency with which they can manipulate themselves and others. I always implore people to study psychology, regardless of their career and life interests; studying and mastering the science of psychology

---

5   Unless somehow the punishment and pain are associated with pleasure and reward...we will deal with this concept more in the chapter on learning.

6   There are, however, personalities that seem to thrive on being controlled.

Literally, the study of the soul

allows one to master the most important tool they have in their possession: the Soul.

Many Western psychologists have expounded on this subject of self-mastery, however it is amongst the ancient civilizations of the world that we find the earliest examples of systems established to accomplish this very task. These processes are found in the form of rites and rituals amongst the various cultures of the non-Western world. Continually in existence as far back as history can record, spiritual growth and initiation has provided societies with a structure for human development, and thus a means through which to develop healthy and thriving societies. What does this have to do with a discussion on practical psychology? In a word: everything.

As stated earlier, psychology is the focused field of study designed to detail all aspects of human beingness, for the purpose of mastering and manipulating it when necessary. If psychology were discussed and understood like this on an everyday basis, many would become defensive, based on the use of the word "manipulating." To think of psychology as a science of manipulation, frames it as an active and strategic knowledge, complete with practical tools. This aspect of psychology is easily demonstrated, yet, it is rarely pointed out in this way, so we hardly think about it in these terms.

One exception, of course, is when you meet someone in a social context and they reveal to you that they are a psychologist and you immediately hide your eyes and say "Are you gonna analyze/manipulate me?" What helped me to take the initial sting out of the word "manipulation" is realizing that it is simply and literally, the handling (manus – Latin for hand) of something for the purpose of influencing its use, condition, state, or functioning.

In the world of psychology, we are constantly manipulating things. As researchers, we manipulate variables and conditions in order to measure the influence of one thing on another; as clinicians, we manipulate the thoughts, speech, emotions, perspective and behaviors of our clients in order to help them to become more functionally effective in their day to day lives; as industrial/organizational psychologists, we work with organizations and corporations to help improve productivity, efficiency, and effectiveness by manipulating their current work-flow models, etc.; as neuropsychologists, we manipulate the brain, seeking to understand and master how brain stimulation and neurochemistry impacts and alters thought, emotions, speech and behavior patterns.

Many find nothing wrong with hiring a clinical psychologist to overcome depression; this is manipulation. The psychologist, thus employed, is trained to manipulate the person's thought processes, their behavior, and ultimately their emotional state, through the use of various psychological tools and techniques (i.e., therapy). In the example of depression, these tools are employed for the purpose of alleviating the depressed feelings and restoring "normal" levels of energy and motivation, and their related thoughts of productivity and hopefulness. The psychiatrist does the same thing, except their major tools are prescription medications in the form of psychotropic drugs.

This is an abbreviated scope of Western or "modern" psychology. This approach is highly effective at certain things, and severely lacking in others. Like most rigid paradigms, there is an entire world that exists beyond its boundaries. If this world ever appears, it is considered an anomaly and either reabsorbed to conform with the paradigm, annihilated, or it causes the paradigm to shift, forcing it to include the presence of something new.

An anomaly related to the field of modern psychology is found/created by simply dealing with the literal meaning of the word. Psychology has the common suffix

Literally, the study of the soul

"-logy," which we find to mean "the study of." The prefix "psych-" comes from the Greek "Psyche," which loosely means "the soul," and comes from the story of Psyche and Eros. Thus giving us "the study of the soul."

Symbolically, this story represents the soul's journey into the flesh and the many temptations to remain limited by the physical state. The soul is provided opportunities to prove itself worthy of return to its heavenly state, and once demonstrated, the soul earns its wings (this is the Egyptian "Ba"), which allows consciousness to travel between heaven (spirit) and earth (the body). I have similarly interpreted the relationship between Shu, Nut, and Geb in the Kemetic (Egyptian) philosophy, to symbolize the need and ability to unify our higher and lower selves. I believe the following image to be the symbolic encoding of how, through self-discipline and control of the breath (Shu), we are capable of reuniting our spiritual selves ("Heaven"; Nut[7]) and our physical selves (Earth; Geb).

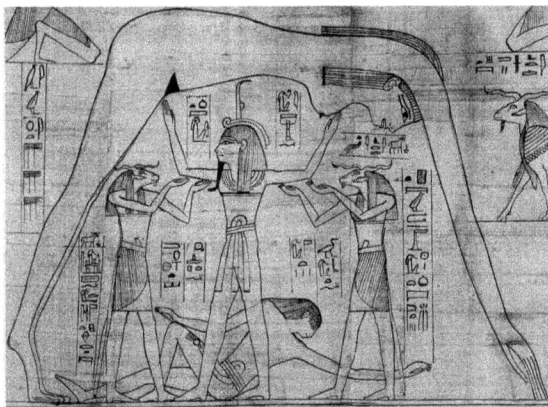

Again, from this perspective, psychology is most accurately defined as "the study of the soul," and provides techniques and processes designed to maximize and actu-

7   Nut is not typically interpreted to represent our spiritual selves by modern Kemetic/Egyptian philosophers, I have come to see the correlation of her heavenly representation with our spiritual selves especially in the context of her relationship with Geb and Shu.

alize its inherent potential. Imagine viewing the various divisions of psychology as divisions of your own soul; then imagine a step-by-step protocol for awakening and making practical those latent gifts and talents. This is how the ancients viewed and practiced psychology, and this is how we shall embark upon the selected topics explored throughout the remainder of this manual. In this manner, the discipline of psychology becomes an outline for a rites of passage program; a process designed to improve the human condition by manipulating one's self-perception, and by developing practical tools for navigating reality. In all subjects, as previously stated, we will highlight the concepts from both the Western and the non-Western worldview. This approach gives us the advantage of emerging with a well-rounded perspective of the topic, as well as the ability to practically apply this knowledge to our daily endeavors.

This book can be viewed as a kind of "Owner's Manual", providing the reader with an opportunity to better "understand and use themselves," on a daily basis, and specifically as part of a larger collective of people, unified towards a common goal. This manual is geared towards identifying psychological principles and concepts most valuable to those interested in organizing behind social and political causes, both as leaders and those who choose to follow. Again, psychology as a discipline, is perhaps the most important of them all.

By taking this practical approach to psychology, it is my hope that much light will be shed on the topics explored, and that a new found understanding, appreciation and desire to learn more about psychology will be awakened in the reader. The study of the soul, if made priority, opens the way for all other subjects to be mastered.

Chapter 3
Socially just...

Social justice as a concept and practice was made necessary by the widespread injustice experienced by the majority of people on the planet. These injustices take many forms, but seem to find a common link in the system of racism/White supremacy. In all areas of people activity, including economics, education, entertainment, labor, law, politics, religion, sex, and war/counter-war, you will find that each of the dividing lines are drawn with a colored pencil. For example, when you explore economic injustice, and you identify the gender-gap regarding wages, you will find that even within the respective gender categories, there is an even greater disparity that exists along the color-line. When you look at the wars that have taken place on this planet, you will find that the most horrific, and devastating versions are those waged against non-White peoples/nations by White peoples/nations. This is true whether we are speaking of the "war on drugs," or the Vietnam, Korean, or the various and on-going wars for control of resource rich African nations. Education-based disparities are also distinguishable by race; more so than social economic status and parent education levels.

These disparities do not speak to the potential nor to the innate attributes of non-White peoples, but instead, identify how the system is skewed in such a way that it supports the progress of Whites, while actively stifling the progress of non-Whites. The mechanisms for impeding the progress of non-Whites can be difficult to identify because they are constantly changing form and becoming more sophisticated as the system continues to mature and refine itself. Mr. Neely Fuller, Jr. spoke directly to this occurrence when he defined what we now know as the *4 Stages of Racism: Establish, Maintain, Expand,* and *Refine.* Refinement is the mechanism by which the tools of racism/White supremacy are adjusted, in order to render them more efficient, effective, less apparent, and even more acceptable by those who are negatively affected by their use. In line with this concept, Amos Wilson often stated that the most effective systems of oppression, are those that associate oppression with a sense of progress and freedom, placing an invisible yoke on its victims.

The field of psychology presents the most progressive, important, and effective tools used to perpetuate systems of injustice, including the system of racism/White supremacy. In the May/June, 1998, issue of *Psych Discourse (vol. 29, Nos. 5 & 6)* Dr. Asa Hilliard explores the presence of racism/White supremacy in psychology, providing the following, insightful analysis:

> If psychology is to be a healing discipline, then the discipline must be purged of its connections to (and participation in) structures of domination through the use of the political categories of race, as if they had biological validity.
>
> It is easy to document the fact that many influential psychologists have used, and many still use, the discipline of psychology to create the structure of racism/white supremacy, to maintain and to legitimize it. Just because psychologists appear to follow a scientific protocol does not at all guarantee valid non-racist practice.
>
> Psychology, as we know it, emerged during the time of slavery, colonization and segregation/apartheid. More important, like other academic disciplines during that time, prominent psychologists, a majority, played major roles in establishing the beliefs and behaviors that created the struc-

Socially just...

tures of domination, in the United States and indeed in the world ...(pp. 8 & 9)

The importance of psychology, when it comes to its impact on our day-to-day lives, cannot be overstated. Psychology specifically, and the social sciences generally, in regards to their ability to define mental health, and its role in the determination of how to address, treat, and correct the same, gives it almost an unchecked ability to determine how people can and will live their lives. A person who does not understand this aspect of psychology, will likely misunderstand much about life in general.

Wilson also spoke of how important it is to see psychology as a political tool for the creation of social justice, and how it was imperative for American African (Black) psychologists to develop a perspective and system of psychology that is designed to address the different perspectives of normalcy held by oppressors, as compared to the perspectives of the oppressed. He noted that oppressors need to define "normal" in favor of their own unjust behaviors toward the oppressed populations; thereby making the behaviors and concepts of the oppressed, that directly oppose their continued domination, abnormal and signs of mental illness. Draeptomania and Daesthesia Aethiopicus are excellent examples of this phenomenon.

He furthers the discussion by identifying how the field of psychotherapy is full of theories and practices designed to get people to adjust their own levels of functioning, to match the standards set by society as a whole. This would be okay if society was not calibrated and based on the need to maintain White superiority over non-White people (racism). Encouraging non-White people to modify their discomfort and "maladaptive behaviors," which are largely a result of living in a racist society, to come more into accordance with the norms of a society based in racism, is asking them to settle more deeply into their psy-

Practical Psychology 101

chosis and compliance with a psychotic "norm." Although this compliance may prove beneficial to their "survival" and "progress" in society, it is still quite detrimental to their sense of self. This is evidenced by those who modify their hair from it's natural state in order to avoid, or at least decrease, the race-based discrimination documented in the hiring practices of many companies. If this were only a superficial modification, it could be considered a non-consequential strategy used to skillfully navigate this racist obstruction; on the contrary, many actually buy into the psychologically dangerous and damaging lies claiming European features and attributes to be more professional, and therefore more valuable than those of Africans, Asians, and other non-White peoples. The higher success rate of being employed, enjoyed by those who accommodate and assimilate to this perspective, provides the concrete evidence and reward necessary for the seemingly endless perpetuation of this perspective and practice.

There have been several attempts made to address the inherent racism found in the field of psychology, including the development of organizations and divisions within organizations, designed to expose, and when possible correct, the harm done by psychological racism. The Association of Black Psychologists (ABPsi) is perhaps the most prominent example of such an organization. Founded in September of 1968 by a group of psychology students, professors, and practicing psychologist, ABPsi is dedicated to the psychological healing of African people, who have been continually served high doses of race-based injustice by the practice and academic discipline of psychology.

In 1999, Robert L. Williams, former president of ABPsi, stated in a letter written to the then president of the APA, Richard Suinn, that ABPsi was organized to:

1) promote & advance the profession of African Psychology

Socially just...

2) influence and affect social change and

3) develop programs whereby psychologists of African descent can assist in solving problems of Black communities and other ethnic groups.

Williams continues by stating that the APA:

1) had not related to the needs of the Black community

2) had used the Black community as a resource for research

3) had never utilized its own resources to assist the Black community in overcoming the effects of White racism; and

4) had failed to utilize its resources to eradicate racism within the White community.

For fifty years, ABPsi has been at the forefront of a movement to apply pressure on the American Psychological Association, as well as the American Psychiatric Association, to address and correct the lasting legacy of racism/White supremacy found in their historical existence and practices. In this same letter, Robert Williams made requests of the APA in the following **Petition of Concerns**:

1) Officially endorse the <u>Kerner Commission's Report of Civil Disorders</u>

2) Develop or implement policies related to the Black Community

3) Bring to bear its resources to finding solutions to the problems of racism and poverty

4) establish a committee to study the misuse of standardized psychological instruments

5) re-evaluate the adequacy of certified training programs in clinical and counseling training programs in terms of their relevance to social problems.

6) recommend to each psychology department steps to be taken to increase the numbers of Black students into their graduate programs

7) consult with representatives of ABPsi to implement and evaluate the progress of the above recommendations.

There was also a six-point statement on testing made by ABPsi and presented to APA, calling for a moratorium, a discontinuation of testing Black children. The six points were statements regarding the negative impact of testing on Black children because testing is used to:

1) label Black children uneducable

2) place Black children in [deficiency-based] special classes

3) potentiate inferior education

4) assign Black children to lower educational tracks than Whites

5) deny Black children higher educational opportunities, and

6) destroy positive intellectual growth and development of Black children.

Although the APA did not comply with every request, the pressure was enough to create changes in a positive and beneficial direction for American Africans. Educators and researchers such as Asa Hilliard were responsible for creating a greater awareness of the injustices found in the area of psychometric assessment. This is the branch of psychology responsible for the creation of psychological instruments used to test intelligence, ascertain personality types, as well as various aspects and degrees of mental illness and mental health.

On the academic side, more American Africans began enrolling and completing graduate programs in psychology. The increased number of American Africans enrolling does not necessarily translate into more beneficial psychologists and perspectives of psychology for American Africans. As Dr. Carter G. Woodson pointed out, it does

Socially just...

more damage if students are being mis-educated, because they are intentionally given the wrong information about themselves and others. This is especially detrimental when African descendants are taught to value the history, culture, and identity of others, more than they value their own. This makes up the bulk of the education process in the conquered world, especially amongst colonized people. This is why school-based instruction in Gambia, West Africa, is done in English; and why school-based instruction in the United States honors and celebrates enslavers of Africans as heroes. I have coined this phenomenon: "assault with a deadly curriculum."

We also find an increase in the number of institutions providing courses designed to address the existence of racism/White supremacy in both the field of psychology, and in society at-large. Courses like "African Psychology," "Black Psychology," and "Multicultural Counseling," give voice to perspectives that differ from the mainstream, and so-called "normal" definition of psychology. I tell my students of multicultural counseling that "racism makes this course necessary." If this is the class designed for us to explore the cultural differences that play a role in how counseling services are both delivered and received, then it must mean that the courses labeled "counseling psychology" deal with the same, except from a predominately White perspective. A simple review of the major theories and theorists explored in a typical psychology book will verify this point beyond the shadow of a doubt.

In consideration of the above, we will now enter into our discussion of social justice, and how social justice movements and organizations, in one way or another, are designed to address injustice. To properly begin this discussion, we must define the terms social and justice. Social means "relating to society or its organization." The word justice has many definitions including, but not limited to

Practical Psychology 101

the following:

> The quality of being just; fairness; Conformity to moral rightness in action or attitude; righteousness; The attainment of what is just, especially that which is fair, moral, right, merited, or in accordance with law; The upholding of what is just, especially fair treatment and due reward in accordance with honor, standards, or law; The administration, system, methods, or procedures of law; Conformity to truth, fact, or sound reason;

In order to gain a deeper understanding of the above definitions of justice, I suggest that you take a moment and look up the words used to define the concept, especially: *moral, rightness, righteousness, just, fair, merited, law, reward, honor, standards, conformity, truth, fact,* and, *reason.* You will find that the above definitions are highly subjective, meaning they can be altered and bent to fit particular political orientations, even those that may be damaging to others, and even unjust. This hypocrisy is what led Mr. Neely Fuller, Jr. to develop his own definition of justice, which, in true counter-racist and compensatory fashion, is designed to produce a universally and mutually beneficial perspective of justice. His definition is:

> *"Making sure that those who need the most help, get helped the most; and, guaranteeing that no one is mistreated."*

Notice how he makes no mention of law, nor of morality, legal, reasoning, etc. This is intentionally done, in order to, as much as possible, remove those aspects of "justice" that can be manipulated to actually produce injustice. A great example of how "laws" have been constructed and enforced, in order to legally perpetuate injustice are the numerous laws designed to prevent teaching enslaved Africans to read and write. The *Virginia Revised Code of 1819* states, in part:

> That all meetings or assemblages of slaves, or free negroes or mulattoes mixing and associating with such slaves

38

Socially just...

at any meeting-house or houses, &c., in the night; or at any SCHOOL OR SCHOOLS for teaching them READING OR WRITING, either in the day or night, under whatsoever pretext, shall be deemed and considered an UNLAWFUL ASSEMBLY; and any justice of a county, &c., wherein such assemblage shall be, either from his own knowledge or the information of others, of such unlawful assemblage, &c., may issue his warrant, directed to any sworn officer or officers, authorizing him or them to enter the house or houses where such unlawful assemblages, &c., may be, for the purpose of apprehending or dispersing such slaves, and to inflict corporal punishment on the offender or offenders, at the discretion of any justice of the peace, not exceeding twenty lashes." (1 Rev. Code, 424-5.)

Social justice movements tend to address their respective causes based on one or some of the above definitions, both in favor of how justice is represented in society, as well as in challenge to how justice is itself, dealt with unjustly. This is a very important notion because many feel that "justice" has not been served when a police officer is found "not guilty" after murdering an unarmed victim. People feel that justice has not been served because the killing was wrong, but courts rule that within the context of "the law" no crime has been committed, therefore they are not convicted. Again, according to the usual definitions, "justice" is the correct application of the law, which is a separate issue from determining the correctness of these laws.

The following five points, outlined by Sue & Sue in their *Multicultural Counseling* textbook, illustrate how the social justice perspective is used to gain a new view on existing issues, by shifting the focus from the victims to the system, and the context within which they both exist:

1) The locus of the problem may reside in the social system (other students, hostile campus environment, alienating curriculum, lack of minority teachers/staff/students, etc.) rather than in the individual.

39

Practical Psychology 101

2) Behaviors that violate social norms may not be disordered or unhealthy.

3) The social norms, prevailing beliefs, and institutional policies and practices that maintain the status quo may need to be challenged and changed.

4) Although remediation is important, the more effective long-term solution is prevention.

5) Organizational change requires a macrosystems approach involving other roles and skills beyond the traditional clinical one.

Using these five points to inform your view of everyday injustices not only empowers your analysis, but also provides a better way to frame the issues at hand. The first step is to shift the focus away from the individual by refusing to assume that the individual is the source of the problem. People are often identified as the issue, and a pass is given to the system in which they are produced. A profound example is the pond where fish are found to have deformities. After pulling a few deformed fish from the water, an astute person should realize that the environment may be contaminated, thereby causing the observed malformations. This is the same for society. If a certain type of person or condition is constantly being produced, then there must be something in society producing it, intentionally, haphazardly, or in total ignorance.

We have heard many politicians, educators, law enforcement officers, and mental health professionals attempt to explain behaviors and conditions as if they are innate to the individual, totally devoid of the historical context, while ignoring the role of society-at-large. An op-ed column published by the *Baltimore Sun*, authored by a *Towson University* professor, provides an excellent example of this shift of responsibility from society to the victims.

In this article, the author claims that the issue of

Socially just...

escalated violence found in Baltimore is because of the large number of fatherless households found in certain communities. As I read this column, I was inspired to write and submit a rebuttal, which was never published (of course). In my response, I took the social justice approach, related to the first point outlined above, showing that the issue is not rooted in the individual households, but within the systematic experiencing of violence by American Africans in the city of Baltimore, from enslavement to the present. It's a known fact that Baltimore was one of the largest "slave ports" in North America, and that the enslaved Africans dragged through this portal, experienced excessive levels of "legal" misery and violence, with little to no experience of true justice. This violence extends into the modern day mass incarceration of American Africans, which is an extension of slavery, and to the consistent experiences of morally-deprived actions committed by those who are designated to uphold justice. This mass incarceration, death-, and brutality-by-cop, and the history of slavery, are just a few of the many society-based issues leading to single-parent households and violence in Baltimore.

The next point shows the error of assuming that a behavior or ideology is abnormal or unhealthy, simply because it violates what is considered "normal" by society. It also challenges the notion that all "social norms" adhered to and promoted by society are in fact healthy, beneficial, and ordered. The word *normal* in this context only means that it is statistically what the majority of people are doing or at least profess to be doing, not that what they are doing is correct, natural, or healthy. For example, it is "normal" for people to have leprosy in a leper colony, whereas in the overall population, it's a disorder, an abnormality. Similarly, in a system dominated by racist/White supremacist ideologies, it is "normal" for laws, and the enforcement of the same, to favor White people, and to be geared towards harming non-White people. This is why race-based discrepancies in criminal sentencing still exist.

It may actually be a sign of mental health to challenge these "norms." As mentioned earlier, Amos Wilson often said it was necessary for American Africans to be mentally unhealthy in order to maintain the current system of injustice. He furthered this point by identifying how modern methods of psychotherapy and counseling are designed to make American Africans more complicit and in-line with the unhealthy societies in which they find themselves; in other words, the system is designed to promote conformity with itself, even at the cost of one's own mental well-being. This is done by "normalizing" pathology, and making healthy, oppositional reactions to the disordered conditions, a sign of illness and disease.

The third point addresses the fact that existing policies and norms may need to be challenged and/or changed. It's the next logical step in our recognition that there may be an issue in society as opposed to the individual, and that individual behaviors may not necessarily be faulty, simply because they contradict societal norms. To have a critical eye when evaluating society, social systems, and the people who create and benefit from them, allows for the proliferation of an analytical mind, a discerning view, and hopefully, a more accurate set of conclusions being drawn as a result. The foundation of many social justice movements, from the founding of African Lodge #1 (currently known as Prince Hall Freemasonry) to the recent "March for Our Lives," rest upon this principle of challenging existing "norms;" identifying how these so-called norms are beneficial to some individuals and groups, but remain intentionally injurious, and unjust to the majority of people. The Black Panther Party, MOVE, SNCC, UNIA, Rainbow/PUSH, and countless other social justice movements were unapologetically designed to push back against this society-level normalization of injustice.

The fourth point is designed to distinguish our orientation from one of reactionary movements to proactive organizing. This means that social justice movements do best when they are organized and functioning with the intention of establishing justice, outside of the presence of a crisis. The perpetual crisis-state of oppressed communities and populations makes this all but impossible. This has been the case since the days of colonialism and chattel enslavement. Being reactionary means being dependent on something occurring, either by surprise or in full expectation, in order to become active. This inhibits the development and use of well thought-out activities, and instead, promotes more "knee-jerk" reactions as the primary approach for engaging one's environment. This means external factors determine when and how these actions take place, more than predetermined strategies. Think about when you are hungry and as a result, go to the grocery store. Your purchasing decisions in this state are likely to be based on hunger, and likely to differ if you were not hungry and/or had a preplanned grocery list.

Being responsive, as opposed to reactive, and therefore in a prevention mind-state as opposed to "treatment" mind-state, grants the luxury of considering multiple angles from a calmer, more stable, emotional disposition. As a point of observation, the development of healthy social systems is not as effective if attempted from a place of injury or illness, but is best from a place of maximum and optimal well-being. This is like a person who daily addresses their immune health by eating foods and taking supplements that support immunity, compared to the person who, because they do not do these things, is battling the flu. This second person is now trying to get rid of the flu, from the miserable position of having it. I'll take prevention over secondary and tertiary intervention any day.

Practical Psychology 101

Prevention will make it less likely that issues of injustice will ever show up and survive in the first place.

The fifth and final notion is that the approach should be macro, meaning on the highest levels possible. Instead of trying to address the injustices solely on the individual levels, energies should also be directed towards the higher levels of society where policies and cultural determinants of "normal" are being created and perpetuated. Macrosystem approaches include addressing media, politics and politicians, education, economic structures, labor-based disparities, health inequity, hiring practices, etc. Unfortunately, whilst in the middle of a battle against injustice, it is very difficult for those who are suffering, to see beyond the immediate concern, in order to catch a better understanding of the situation at hand. This is the case even when a broader perspective is shown to those who are being victimized. There may be an intellectual acknowledgment of the macro-level issues, yet, the situation itself requires one to focus on the immediacy of the problems at-hand, thereby monopolizing their energies.

This is illustrated by a person whose wooden canoe has sprung a leak. They are wise to be more focused on surviving the pending sinking of their boat, by figuring out how to bail out the water. They should rightfully scoff at anyone offering a critique of the quality and the brand of canoe they have purchased while in the midst of this crisis. However, once they are safe on the river bank, they'd do good to seek out a better brand of canoe, one with a superior level of craftsmanship and design. Until then, it is difficult, and perhaps futile to attempt to put the necessary energy towards understanding the source of their current life-or-death situation. This highlights the importance of having a variety of social justice organizations working to solve the same problem, from many angles. Some can serve on the frontlines, while others are perched away from the immediate problems, and therefore can focus clearly on the development of prevention strategies, and methods for advancing the group beyond their current susceptibility.

Historically speaking, the need for social justice, as it relates to psychology, has been tirelessly fought for by some, and enthusiastically avoided by others. As previously mentioned, social justice movements and organizations are made necessary by the existence of injustice in the form of systemic racism/White supremacy. Therefore, the history of the United States of America is filled with examples of the intentional proliferation of injustice, and the rise of social justice movements designed to combat it. Examples are found in all areas of activity including: economics, education, entertainment, labor, law, politics, religion, sex, and war. Racism/White supremacy has effectively influenced each area with one precise and surgical cut from its most effective tool: the peculiar institution of chattel slavery.

The enslavement of Africans was part of a European-created situation that prompted the construction of an entire system, designed to establish, maintain, refine, and expand their ideas of supremacy. These ideas literally "required" the development of a process for enslaving and further oppressing Africans, the means by which Africans would remain inferior and in bondage, and how to "legally" satisfy the deficiency-based needs of Europeans. The following are examples of how this was manifested, specifically in and by the field of psychology and psychiatry.

Let's first look at the pathologizing of African culture and why this was required. There is a long record of mental health organizations and authorities systematically and individually working to create a negative definition, image and perception of Africans. In the early days of diagnosing psychopathology, there were disorders created to address the obsession that some enslaved Africans had with the idea of freedom. This obsession would sometimes lead the enslaved to seek freedom by running away from the plantation, and/or burning down or otherwise destroying crops and buildings. These "diagnoses," Draeptomania and Daesthesia Aethiopicus, were based on the notion that the "natural," and therefore necessary, condition for Africans was in bondage and under the control of Whites and their systems.

From this perspective, enslavement was said to be a benefit to the enslaved, and Whites were considered a noble group, doing an honorable thing for Africans by enslaving and eventually "civilizing" them. The reality of the situation is that the White enslavers were intentionally perpetuating a crime against humanity, and served as the "poster child" for barbarity and uncivilized behaviors. They often used "science" to support their claims and disposition; unfortunately, the scientists themselves had stakes in the perpetuation of their racist ideology and practices, so they lied and did whatever necessary to maintain and refine the system. For example, scientists claimed:

–Africans were intellectually inferior to Whites—requiring that Africans receive little to no education, or even substandard forms of academic training;

–Africans were more criminal and violent in nature than Whites—requiring that Africans be profiled and treated as criminals, thereby creating a disproportionate rate of incarceration and interactions with criminal justice systems;

–Africans were more sexually-aggressive and promiscuous than Whites—requiring that White women be fearful of and protected against African sexuality, both as potential victims of rape, and as victims of their husbands being seduced by the sexual prowess of African women.

Perhaps the most profound aspect of these made-up characteristics of Africans is that the White population was actually more likely to perpetuate rape, assault, theft,

Socially just...

and other criminal acts against Africans than Africans were against Whites. J. A. Rogers has clearly demonstrated in his three volumes of *Sex and Race* that both White men and women had a strong and aggressive desire for sex with Black bodies, that was often played out with Whites as the initiators and authors of these fantasies made real. Dr. Frances Cress Welsing spelled out, in great detail, the underlying psychology fueling these characteristics and behaviors throughout her book, *The Isis Papers*.

Social justice movements are typically designed to address one or more of these issues, thereby providing several points of alignment between them. W. E. B. DuBois predicted "the problem of the color line" to be the major issue of the 20th century. He was correct as we can clearly see that almost every point was drawn with a colored pencil, making racism the main injustice to be addressed. Psychology, psychiatry, and other mental health related jobs, are the driving force propelling systematic injustice because they are the professions used to justify and create the injustices manifested in all other areas. The social justice perspective and approach becomes a necessity because of this. It is required to correctly define and work towards the manifestation of mental health, amongst the oppressed.

Establishing social justice requires that we identify areas wherein equal access and opportunities have been limited and adversely impacted by laws inhibiting certain groups from learning of, and/or utilizing rights and resources that are guaranteed with relative ease to others. Redlining in the housing market stands as an irrefutable example of such practices. Segregated hospitals and schools also exemplify this practice, especially when these public institutions never became "separate but equal."

An example is the legal battle currently taking place between Maryland-based Historically Black Colleges and Universities (HBCU) and the State of Maryland for an alleged unequal provision of resources to state-run HBCUs, as compared to state-run PWIs (Predominately White Institutions). To some, the discrepancies are obvious, and have existed for a long time, resulting in the crippling of HBCUs and their ability to produce at the same level of PWIs. In spite of this disparity, HBCUs often perform above and beyond expectation and academic standards. Imagine what would happen if the playing fields were leveled. Some say this possibility is actually what motivated the alleged discrepancies in the first place.

In addition to addressing inequities in access and opportunities, social justice programs and organizations focus on issues underlying the creation of disparities in other areas that negatively impact the overall quality of life of oppressed populations, including healthcare and employment. It is very clear that health disparities exist, and serve as a major obstacle to the optimal performance of non-Whites. These barriers produce and/or exasperate existing risk factors including the higher rates of exposure to disease causing agents, and succumbing to chronic illnesses and other health-related variables that decrease quality and length of life. Disparities in employment are directly related to disparities in health, based on the relationship between healthcare access, income, and the provision of high-quality treatment based on levels of coverage. This relationships between race and health outcomes have been thoroughly illustrated by Harriet Washington in her phenomenal book, *Medical Apartheid*.

Social justice programs with an agenda related to acquiring justice in mental health will also consider, and base their platforms on, the need for a socially-just perspective of psychological assessment, diagnosis and treatment. If individual practitioners are wedded to the deficit model, and the structural racism upon which the field of psychology and psychiatry are built, then they are more

Socially just...

likely to perpetuate injustices through their daily practice. This translates into the disproportionate misdiagnosis and subsequent mistreatment of non-White populations. This makes for an almost inescapable loop of economic-, education-, and legal-based hardships. To misdiagnose, is to set one up for mistreatment, to mistreat is to leave the actual issues unaddressed, while creating new harm; this is often labeled "benign neglect" or treated as the result of *implicit bias*, but may actually be intentionally employed for more sinister purposes.

Finally, social justice-based programs and organizations, the good ones at least, will also have as a focus, the holistic understanding of both the problem and the necessary solutions. This means that issues are addressed at all levels, including: individual, family, community, society, nation, and cultural; and from a multitude of angles including: economics, education, entertainment, labor, law, politics, religion, sex, and war/counter-war. This makes it less likely that subtle issues will be overlooked, and more likely that the approach to remedy the ills of injustice are thorough and comprehensive. You will find that the social justice movements and organizations that have had the greatest levels of success, are those that incorporate as many areas of human activity as possible. Within this select few, the movements that experience the greatest success, are those that seek to improve the overall psychological state of the victims of systemic injustice. This is more than a notion and is the reason why this manual exists. We must begin to understand our problems to be holistic and systemic, and therefore create our solutions based on this understanding.

The soul, of which psychology is the study of, is the all pervasive aspect of human beingness, that when suppressed, leaves one susceptible to all sorts of ills, and when strengthened, affords the luxury of empowerment, self-determination, and sovereignty; this translates into overall health, and general well-being.

The ancient African-centered perspective of social justice is one that was not separate from the existing structures of society, meaning, the principles associated with social justice are what society as a whole was based upon. This is made apparent by the study of the ancient Kemetic (Egyptian) concept of Maat, and the ancient Yoruba concept of Iwa Pele. Both acknowledge the underlying righteousness of nature, which is based upon reciprocity, justice, equality, order, balance, health, wellness, love and prosperity. The natural cycle of life does not take without giving, nor does it create disorder by its action and inaction. The natural order of creation works to restore anything that is depleted, and does so without further disrupting the order that exists outside of that which is being restored. This is justice.

The most profound example of this natural phenomenon is the exchange of oxygen and carbon dioxide between plant life and mammals. It is also observable in the equal duration of night and day, governed by the earth's movements as it relates to the position of the sun and moon. The notion of natural justice, upon which society-based justice was built, is further exemplified by the existence of natural predators and their natural prey; the absence of either would eventually produce an imbalance that will impact all other aspects of creation. This is the profundity and depth of this call to seek and produce justice. It is packaged within the study of the soul, because it is on the soul-level that we must gather the power to make this an objective reality. Practical psychology, is the application of a soul-technology, for the sole purpose of the production of justice. Hence, the need for socially just movements that are grounded, filled with, and based upon psychologically healthy concepts and people.

Chapter 4
Stay woke...

Consciousness, as a popular term, is used to identify a certain level of enlightenment. Unfortunately, within this context, it has taken on a negative connotation with words like "hoteps" and "ankh-right" being used to describe so-called enlightened individuals who are highly hypocritical and perhaps not as enlightened as they pretend to be. It is an assault against the Ancestors of the Nile Valley in East Africa to use such powerful and meaningful terms (Hotep and Ankh) to refer to negative states of being. Each word loosely means "peace" and "life," respectively. How does a person in their right mind use and promote these powerful terms as negative labels? Y'all woke or what?

For the purposes of this manual, consciousness has two basic dimensions: awareness and awakeness. The former, awareness, deals with how perceptive we are to the things and situations taking place both in our internal world as well as the external environment around us. The latter, awakeness, deals with where we are functioning, at any given moment, on the sleep-wake continuum, of which the two extremes are: death and highly stimulated brain activity. For the sake of this chapter, we will individually explore both aspects of consciousness, and provide a discourse on how to practically apply this knowledge in your everyday life, specifically in the context of social justice movements.

Unfortunately, the standard psychological definition and conceptualization of consciousness relies heavily on externally observable behaviors, and is based on a history of psychologists and psychiatrists denouncing consciousness as a subject unworthy of inquiry and study. For example, William James, in his 1904 paper *Does Consciousness Exist?*, dismisses consciousness studies simply because the then current methods of "scientific" investigation were incapable of measuring or otherwise assessing it. Similarly, the father of modern behaviorism and past president of the American Psychological Association, John Watson, also dismissed the study of consciousness, simply because it was not observable and measurable in the ways the discipline of psychology had accepted as valid, or developed the capacity to apply.

In his 1913 article, *Psychology as the Behaviorist Views It*, Watson stated: "The time seems to have come when psychology must discard all references to consciousness." It is very important to understand that psychology, like all other subjects, has a political aspect. In this case, both James and Watson were promoting their own behaviorist school of thought, while simultaneously downplaying other schools, specifically those of psychoanalysis and psychodynamic theories, as championed by Sigmund Freud and Carl G. Jung; both of whom dealt heavily with consciousness and the unconscious aspects of the mind.

The field has relaxed quite a bit in regards to downplaying the presence and value of consciousness research, however, there has yet to be an accepted (valid) method of observing consciousness except via self-report while monitoring brain activity using an EEG or some form of brain imaging technology. These methods of scientific observation are specific to measuring and analyzing the "awake" aspect of consciousness, but can also be used to make certain observations regarding awareness.

When it comes to observing the material of the

unconscious mind, we have the tools of the previously mentioned schools of thought (psychodynamic and psycho-analytic). These include techniques such as: dream interpretation, free association, and the relatively new methods of projective measures, i.e., the Rorschach, Thematic Apperception Test, Sentence Completion Test, House-Tree-Person Drawings, Dream Analysis, etc.

Consciousness, in the awareness sense of the word (pun intended), deals with sensory awareness, direct inner awareness, depths of internal thoughts and feelings (conscious, unconscious, pre-conscious), and finally, and perhaps the most esoteric (mystical), it also deals with our concept of who and what we are, as distinguished from other things and people in our environment (sometimes called "self-awareness").

Dealing first with sensory awareness, we are specifically talking about how aware a person is of their external environment, as it relates to their physical sense organs being stimulated. Before proceeding, I'd like to provide a brief overview of the relationship between sensation & perception. As an easy reminder, I always teach students in my Introduction to Psychology courses that sensation occurs at the sensory organs (eyes, ears, nose, mouth, skin) while perception occurs in the brain. In other words, sensation, when you actually sense something, is literally the stimulation of special cells within a sensory organ, by external energy. Perception is the brain's encoding and interpretation of that stimulation, and is largely based on the context provided by previous experiences, and certain predictive functions of the brain.

In a healthy system, this energetic stimulation (light wave, sound wave, chemical contact, pressure/temperature change) sets off a series of reactions wherein the nerves connected to the sensory organs send a message to the brain, or some part of the nervous system, for interpretation, and eventually, a response or reaction. I say "some part of the nervous system" because there are situations where the stimulation will not go to the brain initially, but instead, stays relatively local (going between the point of contact and the spinal cord) for the purpose of getting an almost instant reflex. This is a safety mechanism and is most readily identifiable when you step on something sharp and your foot immediately pulls back, or when you touch something hot and your hand snatches away, or the moment you smell a toxic gas and immediately stop inhaling, scrunch up your nose and pull away.

In most cases, these reactions are automatic and occur before we have a single thought about the stimulation. It is usually during the reaction that you begin to think things such as "Ewwwww, that stinks!" or "Ouch, what did I step on!" If your body had to wait for your brain to evaluate how hot the stove is when you accidentally touch it before it responds, there would be a lot more people in this world with unnecessarily severe burns. Instead, the body snatches the hand away, without the need for input from the brain, because of a special relationship between our sense organs (of which the skin is the largest), the peripheral and central nervous systems, and our muscles.

Regarding perception, isn't it amazing how two people can see (sense) the exact same thing, from the exact same angle, yet carry a different interpretation of what they are looking at? All things being equal in regards to the strength of their eyes, you would think that two people looking at a furry little Chow (dog) would see the same cute animal; not so. Some will view this creature and "see" a vicious beast ready to attack, and will immediately go into a fear response; while others will view the dog and "see" an adorably cute creature that makes them want to pick it up, pet it, and allow it to lick their face. Remember, they are both seeing the same dog, at the same time from the same perspective, it is only their perception of the dog that differs.

So what is this powerful, reality shaping, and sometimes reality shifting phenomenon called perception? By definition, perception is the result of detecting, processing and interpreting information. In modern psychology, perception is almost always linked to sensation, meaning the information being detected, processed and interpreted comes from the stimulation of receptor cells within the sensory organs. There is, however, a large body of literature[8] examining what we know as ESP, or extra-sensory perception. This refers to the phenomenon of perceiving things without direct stimulation of sensory cells and organs.

This controversial field of study is housed within the larger subject of parapsychology (literally meaning "beyond [the boundaries of] psychology"). I suspect it is considered "para-" only because it exists beyond the current paradigm and its acceptable means of "scientific" investigation. It has been "explained away" by modern psychology as simply a matter of chance, deception, and grand schemes akin to those of a stage magician.[9] While there are many charlatans who pretend to have psychic abilities, there are also those who have demonstrated, beyond a doubt, their gifts and talents which surpass those of the typical human being. Again, much of the controversy exists due to the fact that the modern scientific methods of investigation have failed to satisfy their own requirements of proof; this doesn't mean that "proof" is absent and therefore, ESP is non-existent. In the words of Sam Jackson's character on *The Boondocks*, Gin Rummy, "The absence of

8   Much of this research took place at the Standford Research Institute (SRI) and Duke University.
9   Uri Geller caused a great amount of tension for scientists trying to prove/disprove the existence of parapsychological phenomenon, specifically telekinesis, telepathy, and clairvoyance.

evidence is not the evidence of absence." We must remember there was a time not long ago when Western "science" locked people away in the horrid conditions of "insane asylums" and "treated" pathology by driving ice-picks through their orbital sockets in order to sever brain tissue in the early form of what is now called a pre-frontal lobotomy.

The most sound explanation, used to debunk ESP as a factual occurrence, is that of "subliminal stimulation" which leads to "subliminal perception." This is when a person's sensory organs are activated by external energy, but it occurs beneath the threshold of their conscious awareness. Meaning, the person has actually sensed something without knowing (being conscious) that they have sensed it. Thus they are actually perceiving the sensation without awareness of the sensation, and thus the perception is not "extra-sensory" but is truly based on sensory stimulation.

There have been many experiments wherein people are exposed to sounds that are too low for them to consciously hear, but later, they demonstrate they have been influenced by that sound. Or instances where people are presented with visual stimulation that is moving too quickly for them to consciously sense, yet they demonstrate that the information was detected and processed (perceived) sometimes through biofeedback like increased heart rate, or rate of breathing, or some indication of stress, arousal, or any number of basic autonomic nervous system responses or feedback. We are regularly exposed to this type of subliminal stimulation, and of course it typically happens without us ever realizing it. For evidence, pay attention to the background of your favorite sitcom or movie. There is sure to be a recognizable product floating around somewhere. It can be the glowing apple on the back of a laptop, or the *Batman Vs. Superman* billboard found in the background of *I Am Legend*, a movie starring Will Smith,

Stay woke...

that opened in theaters back in 2007.[10]

There is a famous magician, Derren Brown, who performed an elaborate trick on two London-based marketing agents, proving they are susceptible to their own methods. He used subliminal stimulation to subtly influence the type of picture they would later draw.[11] This phenomenal example demonstrates how effective subtle manipulation can be, and it also demonstrates an aspect of awareness called *selective attention*. Selective attention is when we focus on specific stimulation from our environment, at the expense of not focusing on all other stimulation. In other words, it is when we are only paying attention to the phone in our hands as we walk across the parking lot, and not the car that is backing out of the parking space two vehicles ahead. Typically, this selective attention serves a protective function and allows us to not be overwhelmed by the extreme amount of environmental stimulation and information we are constantly being exposed to on a daily basis. However, as demonstrated in the parking lot example, it can also be hijacked by distractions and position us for great harm.

Stop reading for a few moments and pay attention to all of the sights, sounds, smells, tastes, and other forms of sensory stimulation taking place in and around you as you read. Prior to taking the time to focus on it, you may or may not have been aware of the existence of all of the things you just observed. Had you been consciously focusing on them, you may have been overwhelmed by sensory overload, or you may have never been able to get past the first sentence on this page because you would have been too cognitively distracted to focus on the words and comprehend their meaning.[12] The thing about selective

10   A full nine years before "Batman Vs. Superman" was released.
11   The experiment is fascinating and can be viewed in its entirety at: https://youtu.be/YQXe1CokWqQ
12   In some hypnosis induction techniques, sensory overload is

attention is that it does not totally cancel out all other stimulation; instead, it simply puts everything else into the background, freeing your mind from having to consciously (as in with your awareness) process the data.

A very good illustration of selective attention, the unconscious storage of information, its recall and utility at a later time, is found in the television series *Psych.* In one of the early episodes we find a young "Shawn" sitting in a diner with his father. His father is drilling him on *situational awareness*, testing his ability to recall very specific details about things found around the diner. The episode returns to the present day adult "Shawn" who is now pretending to be a psychic while assisting police and FBI agents to solve crimes. In reality, he has developed his sensory awareness to the point of having a "photographic memory," and is able to return to the "snap shot" in order to consciously process all the information that he has received. He has a clear advantage over most because of this ability to return to the background data, and his desire to actually put it to use.

This skill is directly related to what, in the world of psychological testing, we call *visual acuity*; defined as a measure of how well a person is capable of visually sensing and perceiving things in their environment. This can get tricky because, as stated earlier, perception is highly subjective and heavily dependent upon what other data are stored in the brain/mind as it relates to the present stimulation and situation. If a person has been attacked by a dog, then their perception of a "nice" dog will be colored by this earlier trauma. Contrarily, if a person has grown up, since birth, with loving dogs, then their perceptions will be colored by that experience. Thus, if I am evaluating a person's visual acuity by showing them a picture of the inside of a

---

used to render the individual more receptive to the hypnotic suggestions.

car door, and the door is "missing" a handle to roll up the window (it's an old school car...bear with me 80s and 90s babies), we may run into some issues of validity, based on the presumed "norm" of people's experiences.

To elaborate further: an individual whose family may own a "hooptie," which has always had a pair of vice grips in place of the handle to manipulate the window, may not acknowledge a "handle" as being "missing," but may instead say there is a tool, the vice grips, missing; or perhaps the incense tree hanging from the rear view mirror is missing. Either of these responses would score them a zero (0) for this particular item. Although they are not wrong, their answer is incorrect as far as the test is concerned. This example is a slight altering of a real item on a real intelligence test. I have seen many children miss points because of the culturally-limited features of many of these test items, making it clear to me that some of these tests are actually reporting biased scores.

In a 1970s debate[13] between Drs. Frances Cress Welsing and William Shocklee, Shocklee often referred to his report in the Phi Delta Kappa magazine, *The Kappan*, in which he discusses the intellectual inferiority of American Africans, while simultaneously citing the superiority of American Africans on measures such as visual acuity. He failed to realize, or at least did not acknowledge how important visual acuity is to overall intelligence, a fact that was later evidenced by the inclusion of this category in the tools used to measure intelligence. This aspect of intelligence contributes greatly to *emotional intelligence*, "street smarts," "common sense," and "social interactions;" all forms of intelligence that go well beyond the ability to retain and retrieve facts, information, and data. In fact, neuroscientists are now acknowledging visual acuity to be at the core of most, if not all, perceptual abilities. This is

---

13   https://www.youtube.com/watch?v=V-9jtRx5iGk

because of the need for a contrast between two things, in order to sense and perceive anything.[14]

Returning to our discussion on selective attention, we find that the background data being screened out, is dealt with in many ways. One perspective says that dreams serve the purpose of processing all of this background data that we did not necessarily pay attention to or consciously process while awake. This is known as the *information processing theory* of dreams. It's kind of like having a mental file clerk that waits until the office is closed (the person is asleep) before processing and filing all of the work from the day.

This is why, according to this theory, a person will have dreams semi-related to certain experiences they had while awake. Some will even have dreams related to what is actually going on around them while they are sleeping.[15] The dreams will sometimes deal with off-shoots of actual conversations or otherwise related information, in a manner that does not directly match what actually occurred but is relevant in many ways.

Sometimes we move rapidly through the waking state of our daily lives, and will often misplace or neglect to do something. In cases like this, people will sometimes "find" their lost keys or "remember" to do what they were neglecting, all while dreaming. This may cause them to wake up immediately to complete the neglected task, or go retrieve their keys from where they have been lost, or the person may wake up in the morning with no recollection of the dream and complete the task or "miraculously" find their keys.

---

14   "This property forms the basis of all cognition, including your capacity to see, hear, feel, think, and pay attention. Without it, the world would have no boundaries and your brain could make no sense of itself or anything outside itself." *Sleights of Mind*, p. 11

15   An example of the merging of the awareness and awakeness aspects of consciousness.

Stay woke...

This is a perfect place to discuss two other theories explaining why we dream, they are: *wish fulfillment* and *messages from other sources*. The wish fulfillment theory was made popular by Sigmund Freud who stated that dreams are but the desires that we suppressed during our waking state. These desires are suppressed because they may go against societal norms, what is socially acceptable, or simply because they contradict our religious or other beliefs that we have accepted and adopted for our lives.

While sleeping, our cognitive ego defenses tend to be more relaxed and thus, allow for the expression of those things that we worked hard (albeit unconsciously) to keep from being expressed while awake. An example of this may be found in sex-related dreams containing acts that are considered "taboo," or where we behave in ways that are contrary to our "nature," yet reflect how we truly desire to be (i.e., a typically passive person may dream of being aggressive or assertive with a boss, spouse, or co-worker).

Dreams have long been thought of as the soul's continued journey into another "realm" or dimension, for the purpose of retrieving and or sending information that is beyond the scope of your mind when awake. From this perspective, the characters in your dreams are the souls of other people who are also dreaming or otherwise disconnected from their bodies (Ancestors, Angels, Spirits, etc.). The experiences and interactions that occur in this state are considered real by any measure of the word, and can prove fruitful to those who are aware of how to use this particular tool of consciousness. Professor James Smalls, in the *Ancestral Voices 2* documentary, states that all the various characters in a dream are actually aspects of the dreamer, cloaked under different identities; therefore, the dream is a sequence of interactions with one's own self, usually for the purpose of resolving an inner conflict.

There are stories of how people use the dream state

Practical Psychology 101

to discover information, plan for actions to be taken upon awakening, communicate messages to others, as well as to explore their own subconscious minds (souls). For example, many people of African descent know that to dream of fish, means someone in the family is pregnant. Dream analysts and interpreters specialize in decoding the symbolism of dreams and relating them to the real life, waking state experiences of their clients. Many applaud the merits of such practices, yet very few understand the mechanisms behind the science.

Returning to the notion of consciousness as a matter of awareness, let's explore the concepts of direct inner awareness and the various degrees of awareness: *preconscious*, *unconscious*, and *nonconscious*. Direct inner awareness is the ability to generate and manipulate perceptions without the stimulation of any of the externally-based sensory organs. In other words, it's the ability of a person to visualize or imagine sights, tastes, smells, sounds, or tactile sensations totally in their own minds and literally have a physiological response consistent with actually hearing, seeing, tasting, touching or smelling it.

This direct inner awareness is part of a very powerful tool called *creative visualization* and is often used during meditation and other manifestation-based practices. There has existed practical exercises designed to increase one's abilities to visualize and imagine, in greater detail, for centuries and perhaps millenia. It requires exceptional amounts of concentration and focus, and selective attention on the internal planes. Constantly being flooded with extreme amounts of external stimulation and the rapid changes that take place within the media (commercials, social media sites, etc.), can decrease our ability to consciously utilize creative visualization, by directly impacting our ability to focus and concentrate. An important characteristic of creative visualization is that it plays an active role in our day-to-day life experiences, albeit in the background, and can create both beneficial as well as detrimental outcomes, depending on what is being entertained and focused upon; this occurs whether we are intentionally employing it or not.

In regards to the stages of consciousness: pre-, un-, and non-, we are talking specifically about degrees of awareness: from incapable of being perceived to total and complete perception on a consistent basis. First, the term non-conscious applies to those internal things that are totally imperceptible; an example is our inability to feel neurons firing in the same way you can perceive your own breathing. Of course it can be observed using machinery and technology such as an fMRI or an EEG, otherwise, it does not happen. Additional examples of non-conscious events include: blood transferring oxygen into cells and removing carbon dioxide and other waste from the cells, the transfer of nutrients from the digested foods via the intestinal lining in the small intestines, immune cells attacking a bacteria in the skin, and most other cellular functions.

Certain mind-altering, or consciousness-altering substances (drugs, natural plants, etc.) are reported to have the ability to bring those non-conscious experiences into the realm of conscious awareness.[16] Some have dismissed these experiences as not being a function of true perception, but simply evidence of drug-induced hallucinations.

Unconscious events are considered to be totally unavailable to our awareness without certain processes that are designed to bring them from beneath the veil.[17] These events tend to be those repressed memories and other experiences and thoughts that, for one reason or another, have been placed beyond the scope of our day-to-day

---

16   See *The Cosmic Serpent* by Jeremy Narby
17   Psychoanalysis

thoughts and awareness.[18] This does not mean they have no effect on our thoughts and actions; on the contrary, they have direct, powerful, and often lasting effects on our lives. It's similar to how we cannot see the vital essence of the air we breath, but directly benefit and are impacted by its presence nonetheless. Another example is how a computer's operating system is not readily detectable on the surface, however, it influences and coordinates all of the active operations taking place within the device.

The final level is preconscious information, which is not active in your "sphere of awareness" but is relatively easy to retrieve and incorporate into your conscious thoughts. Preconscious material is information that you have retained, but are not currently using, and thus, it is stored away, within reach, until it is needed. For example, if I asked you to outline the events of yesterday, if you were not thinking about it prior to me asking, ideally you would be able to retrieve the information with details.

In some cases, a portion of the information may have been repressed and thus stored in the unconscious regions of the mind, making them more difficult (and seemingly impossible) to retrieve, while other aspects come to consciousness effortlessly or with little work. The preconscious mind serves the purpose of keeping "unnecessary" information from cramming the conscious mind, but keeping this info close just in case it becomes necessary.

Let us now briefly deal with *self-awareness,* the aspect of consciousness relating to our identity and the ability to distinguish between ourselves, other people, and things in our environment. Self-awareness is of great importance, especially when you are involved in working with others. I often demonstrate this to my clients by

---

18   The movie "Eternal Sunshine of a Spotless Mind" illustrates the use of the unconscious mind as a repository of repressed memories in a most entertaining way.

showing them the value of being able to distinguish between their "stuff" and someone else's "stuff."

Ask yourself: Whose attitude are you experiencing as your own? Is it the person who just recklessly drove past you during your rush hour commute? Is it that of your significant other with whom you shared a hearty laugh before walking out of the door this morning? Is it an emotion imposed upon you by the news? Recognizing the source of emotions and attitudes allows us to properly ascribe their reason and meaning, and also helps us to let go of unnecessary baggage, i.e., other people's stuff.

Being able to reflect on your own life, understanding what motivates and drives you, how others perceive and experience you, and yes, even how all of your life's events have shaped you into the person that you are today (*narrative identity*), is an empowering process leading towards a greater sense of self-awareness. Intentionally developing self-awareness requires an advanced understanding of what your "Self" actually is. We will cover more on this later, for now let me point out that many of us have yet to distinguish between our "person" and our "Self," which is a major factor in being self-aware and becoming a masterful human. The "person" is your conditioned state, and is shaped by your upbringing, race, culture, parents, birth order, gender, etc. The "Self" is that part of you that is beyond conditioning; the part that represents your highest, most powerful, traits and characteristics.

This knowledge is especially useful when organizing and participating in social justice movement-related activities. There are two related concepts known in social psychology as *group think* and the *herd mentality*. These terms describe when a critical mass of individuals think, feel, and/or behave in a similar, and close to exact, manner.

This occurs with or without the realization that the group is synchronized in such a manner. There are various means of intentionally and unintentionally achieving this goal, all of which are related to identity, conditioning, emotions, and the other aspects of psychology explored in this manual. It happens more often than not, and in very subtle, and highly sophisticated ways. Gaining a greater understanding of this point, is the main reason behind the publication of this text.[19]

The world of sports provides us with invaluable and almost unlimited examples of this phenomenon in both positive and negative forms. Think about how many people, fans (fanatics), actually wear the "uniform" of the people playing the game, although they themselves are neither playing, nor an official part of the team. Where else do you know of people wearing the uniform of another profession, for recreation, outside of Halloween and acting?

Recall the news stories of rowdy fans literally rioting in the streets of their town, when the home-team wins the championship. Observe the language used when one discusses "their" team. They often use inclusive terms like "we," and "our," when speaking about how the team is, or will, perform. They have literally identified with being a part of the team, and via this identification, they have also linked their emotions and behaviors to the team's performance and experiences. Need evidence? Just pay attention to how upset and/or joyful people become, based on the outcome of ballgames.

The same can be said about leaders, celebrities, socio-political causes, governments, nations, one's race, gender, or sexual orientation. *The Third Reich* is infamous for their uncanny ability to take this concept and scientifically apply it with great efficiency. Joseph Goebbels, through his science of propaganda, was able to influence the masses of German people to believe in whatever they

---

19   See quote by Gustav Le Bon on pg. vi of this book.

deemed necessary for them to believe, in order for the Nazi regime to carry on as planned. For example, the Nazi regime used propaganda to dehumanize the Semites of the Jewish religion, in order to weaken the sense of empathy and compassion the masses of Germans would have for them. This eventually minimized the opposition to their plan to eventually exterminate the Semitic population.

Some equate this strategy to the modern dehumanizing of American Africans via the negative imagery found in media and popular culture; specifically by the use of the terms "nigga," "bitch," and "dog," to describe members of the race. The way that self-awareness plays into all of this is first found in how one defines who and, perhaps more importantly, what, they are. This understanding, when consciously adapted into your belief system, gives you control over your identity and everything else that comes along with how you identify.

Many of us carry both an individual as well as a collective concept of Self; although Industrial and Organizational Psychologist, Dr. Edwin Nichols, has identified where some cultures and races tend to lean more towards one extreme or the other. This matters because it determines the methods required to manipulate the concept of Self–both who and what the Self is.

For example, if an individual leans more towards the collective concept of what the Self is, it will take far less to convince or compel them to unite with others for a cause; instead, much of the energy can be spent influencing what the already existing collective will do. If the person has a more individualized concept of Self, it may be necessary to first get them to align with others, prior to influencing the group towards a particular thought, belief, and/or action. This is done by generating or identifying a mutual need and either a potential threat to the fulfillment of that need, or simply a promise of gaining more access to

Practical Psychology 101

address that need.

Regardless of the orientation, it is very important for those who would like to be less-susceptible to these influences, to become as aware as possible of their individual thoughts, beliefs, emotions, and understandings; the degree to which you are capable of distinguishing yours from those of others, will often determine the degree to which you are able to function relatively independent of other people's stuff.

If, for example, you are in the presence of a nervous individual, because emotions are simply energy-based experiences (see chapter on emotions), it is easy for them to transfer the sense and feelings of nervousness to you. So even though you are not nervous, you may eventually become nervous after having the feeling of nervousness radiating from others. This is the exact same mechanism that burns a person who touches a pot sitting on fire. The energy (heat) is transferred from the fire, to the pot, to your hand. Your hand is not on the fire, hence is not being heated up, nonetheless, the energy is easily transferable by simple contact with that which is radiating the energy.

Many times people will unconsciously (without awareness) accept the feeling as their own, and actually own the emotion. The discerning, self-aware person, will recognize this energy, discern its source to be somewhere outside of themselves, and seek to employ one of many strategies to dissipate, or otherwise master and control the invading energy. The person lacking self-awareness will be more likely to get caught up in it. The ability to be permeated by external energies, such as emotions, is both a gift and a liability. The gift is that it allows us to be empathic and have sympathy towards others. It also makes you capable of sensing, perceiving and thereby properly engaging your external environment. The liability exists to the degree that we are unaware of how to master emotions

Stay woke...

and are ignorant about the origins of the feelings we are feeling, and thus are more susceptible to being affected by them with minimal understanding, and minimal control.

In my model of healthy psychological development, the *A.S.K. Model*, I outline methods for developing self-awareness utilizing self-monitoring alongside other tools. My clients are encouraged to spend significant amounts of time on this stage and receive holistic guidance and skill development exercises towards this end. For the purposes of this current publication, I will simply highlight how the development of this particular skill, and awareness, benefits those engaged in social justice efforts.

Let's use the recent anti-police brutality protests that have taken place after several killings of unarmed or legally armed American Africans by uniformed and off-duty law enforcement officers. In almost every case, the rallies were organized to be peaceful, although the reason for gathering was fueled by great emotion and a sense that an evil and terrible injustice has occurred. At some point during the rally, the heightened emotion began to translate into actions reflecting anger, fear, confusion, frustration, and perhaps even love. From an objective perspective, one could watch as the feelings spread across the crowd, and could easily predict when the behaviors would escalate beyond the rally, changing the gathering into an uprising and/or riot.

In some instances, the emotions of the crowd began to shift as the police presence increased. When the officers appeared in riot gear, stood in formation, and began to employ what are obviously organized tactics and strategies, the gathering protesters slowly began to react in ways reflective of the change in police behavior. In some cases, the police presence is designed to overtly and intentionally intimidate those that are gathered.

Hopefully the intention behind this intimidation

is to deter the likelihood that the crowd will escalate; unfortunately, the intimidation typically has the opposite effect, leading to an escalation of the energy of the crowd. The self-aware person will be able to read and properly perceive the energy of intimidation, and subsequently, the natural "fight, flight, or freeze" reaction taking place in their body. With the proper tools, they will respond as opposed to riding out the reaction, meaning they will have a cognitive as opposed to an emotional motivation for what comes next. The response may vary, and could be to maintain the same level of organization and structure present prior to the riot gear and formations becoming apparent. The response could be an organized retreat. The response could be an organized advancing. Regardless of how it looks, as it will surely look different based on the situation, goals, leadership, and participants, the point is that it is a response and not a reaction. This is the underlying tactic to "non-violent" movements, tactics directly related to the spiritual and meditative philosophies of India and some African cultures; designed to maintain self-control.

Contrary to what some believe, an effective response may actually be emotionally-driven. This is important to point out because some people are confused and believe that in order to respond, one must be emotionless. Ancient wisdom says "Emotions make poor leaders but are excellent servants." In the words of Orlando Jones' "Anansi" character in the *American Gods* television series, "Anger gets sh!t done." The advantage is found in the intentional response, *using* an emotion, over an unintentional reaction *because of* an emotion. It is a known fact that high emotions tend to negatively impact cognitive functioning (i.e., thinking, remembering, perception, etc.). This is observable when someone "snaps" and does not remember what happened once they wake up. Or how in violent crime scenarios, it is often times difficult for the scared witnesses to accurately recall information about the experience.

Self-awareness also plays a major role in what is known as "implicit bias." Implicit bias is a term used to describe when a person unconsciously ascribes meaning to a person or situation, which directly affects the way they interpret and/or interact in the situation. A major and deeply impacting example is how young American African children are often described as being older and more threatening than they actually are, and as compared to their White peers; or how American Africans are thought to have a higher pain threshold by physicians and nurses, therefore, their treatments and complaints are often not given the degree of respect as that given to their White counterparts.

When explained as implicit bias, it seems to be nobody's fault; instead it is labeled an extension of the unjust socialization that takes place within the larger context of society. Described as the result of racism/White supremacy, race-based implicit bias such as this, becomes an example of systemic racism/White supremacy in action, making people equally responsible and accountable for their part of the whole.

The self-aware individual will be able to recognize their own biases towards or against a particular group, individual, and situation. Therapists, counselors, social workers and psychologists are encouraged to deepen their understanding of their own internal biases prior to working with patients and clients, however, I can say, without a doubt, that many never do the work required to uncover and resolve these biases. This is dangerous because the aforementioned professionals are the ones who "determine" an individual's mental health, intelligence, and the degree to which they are capable of functioning in society.

Think about the school psychologist, who has a bias against American African girls. While performing psycho-educational assessments on American African girls, this bias tells the school psychologist that American African girls always have a negative attitude, and that they will not take the test seriously. This will likely impact how the test is administered, which in turn directly impacts the child's performance, and ultimately the interpretation of the results, all in a negative direction.

There are studies showing how the race and culture of test administrators can impact performance on these psychological tests. Many have interpreted this issue to be related to race-based biases. I have personally experienced a situation where a young American African child received an IQ score in the 70s, which is close to what is needed for a designation of "mental retardation." This test was administered by a White female 3 years earlier. I was asked to test the child for their triennial psycho-educational evaluation. The child and I, both being American African males, had a cultural proximity not shared by the previous test administrator; as expected, the child now had an IQ score over 100; which is in the "average" range.

It is not typical, in fact it is uncommon and unlikely, for an individual's IQ to increase by 30 points; definitely not over a matter of three years, unless of course there was something like impaired vision, or some psychological issue inhibiting their ability to perform on the earlier test. The change was so shocking that my evaluation was reviewed by a supervisor for a mistake on my part. It was thought that maybe I had miscalculated somewhere and perhaps incorrectly scored some responses.

When it was all said and done, and they found no errors in the administration and scoring of the IQ test, I simply asked the child how he felt testing with the previous evaluator. The child used terms like "rushed," "confused," "nervous," and "unliked." The child clearly did not have a good experience and felt like the examiner wanted him to get things wrong. He literally said she was mean. As a result of this potentially biased evaluation, the child was placed in Special Education courses to address deficiencies that were not really there. The new, and more accurate evaluation made it possible for us to reevaluate his educational placement, and to establish a program to restore the child's positive self-efficacy, and a healthy and empowered identity, while also placing them in an appropriate educational setting. Imagine how often this occurs.

Now that we have sufficiently covered the "awareness" aspects of consciousness, let's return to take a look at the "awakeness" side of the coin. As mentioned before, brain wave activity, and the behavioral correlations, seem to be the defining features of the awakeness aspect of consciousness, according to modern psychology. In this category of consciousness, a person is considered to be somewhere on the continuum between dead and wide awake..."dead" being the lack of brain activity and self-sustained bodily function, while "wide awake" means having a high level of brain activity, a wide array of bodily functions, and a degree of intentionality behind behaviors.

There are many steps or degrees of awakeness between dead and wide awake, including comatose and sleepy, with defining features like daydreaming and reflexive non-responsiveness. Each step or stage also produces various degrees of work potential and overall human capability, dependence, and independence. Each stage also correlates with a particular pattern of brain waves.

The brain wave patterns with the highest frequency are those categorized as *beta waves*. This level of wakefulness is associated with being wide awake, and a brain that is stimulated and active. We expect to see this level of brain activity in a person who is currently engaged in a task that requires them to socialize, problem solve, manipulate machinery, etc. These are associated with the *waking state.*

Next we find what are called *alpha waves*. These are a step down from beta, although alpha comes before beta in the Greek alpha-bet(a),[20] and are most readily found in the brains of those who are in a relaxed and receptive state. There are some meditation programs and practices that encourage practitioners to seek to experience and maintain the alpha state of mind (brain wave activity), because they believe it to be a superior condition for problem solving, perceptual awareness, and accessing your intuitive and/or creative mind.[21] This actually makes sense when you consider how a quiet mind is more capable of focusing on a single concept as opposed to the highly active mind that may be distracted by the various points of stimulation being entertained (both consciously and unconsciously).

As stated by Henry C. Clausen:[22]

> The Eastern mystics called the silent mind that which is beyond unconditioned thought. It is the same as awareness or esoteric thinking. If we can tap this state of consciousness, then a decision or problem is resolved that seems otherwise insoluble. There in a quiet place where, without effort to derive a logical answer, the supermind speaks—not an objective voice but more an intuitive flash. Similar results occur when we try strenuously to recall a name, an address or a phone number. After conscious efforts are exhausted and in a moment of mental relaxation, the information "pops" into mind without effort.
>
> Many have found that deliberate recourse to this "inner wisdom" in deciding matters of importance is more dependable than objective intellect.

An appropriate analogy follows: Imagine sitting

---

20   Alpha waves were discovered first...

21   "An inspiration comes from the creative level of the mind, the level which must be reached if psychological changes are to take place. You can't contact that level if you are being critically editorial, so you can't get any constructive impressions into that level if you're argumentative about it." - David Seabury, How to Live With Yourself, pp. 13 - 14.

22   Emergence of the Mystical, by Henry C., Clausen, 1981.

Stay woke...

on a yacht, looking over the edge trying to see your reflection in an ocean whose waves are crashing and rolling with great frequency and force. Now imagine trying to see your reflection from a row boat, positioned in the middle of a calm and clear pond. From the yacht, in the ocean, you are not likely to see any semblance of your reflection in the water; in the pond, you will probably catch a glimpse of yourself, the sky above you, and perhaps even be able to see what lies beneath the surface of the water. The same holds true for a still mind.

Notice how calm and peaceful superior martial artists are when engaged in battle. It's almost unreal how they are able to know where the next strike will be aimed and respond appropriately, almost effortlessly. This example shows the intersection between awareness and awakeness, which are independent of each other, but do work together to create the various degrees and configurations of consciousness. I point you to Barry Gordy's movie, *The Last Dragon* for an illustration, specifically, Bruce Leroy's ability to catch the designated arrow while blindfolded.

The next level of brain activity is usually only recorded once an individual has lost consciousness (i.e., fallen asleep, etc.). These are known as *theta waves*. While experiencing the theta pattern, people are usually in a light sleep and are easily awakened. There may be an experience of brief dream-like images, and the person may maintain awareness of their surroundings. People who take naps or go to sleep and remain at this level of brain activity are commonly referred to as "light sleepers." This is a phase of mental receptivity, in which the person is capable of being influenced without their awareness and usually without the ability to resist. Hypnotists work to guide a person into this level of brain activity for the purpose of rendering them more susceptible to influence and hypnotic suggestions.

Practical Psychology 101

Finally, the slowest/lowest level of brain activity are the *delta waves*. These correlate to deep sleep, wherein there is no recollection of dreaming and the individual is difficult to arouse and awaken. As the great philosopher Nasir Jones stated, "...sleep is the cousin of death." At these deep levels of sleep, mimicking a death-like state where many of our bodily functions decrease in activity. This is a regenerative and restorative experience. It is during this level of sleep that the body is able to repair and restore itself from the experiences of the day. The brain is now relaxing and settling down from the large amounts of stimulation it has received and processed throughout the day, and is preparing to start anew once you awaken.

The ancients observed and studied nature to learn more about the life experiences of humans. To watch the night turn into day, and the day turn into night, was and remains an amazing phenomenon. It is directly related to the sleep-wake cycle, as well as the transition between birth-death-rebirth. I have, on many occasion, sat in silent observation as the sun descended beneath the horizon, noticing how all of the natural daylight activities ceased almost immediately once the sun was no longer visible. The creatures and insects of the day fall silent almost instantly. Their movements are no longer observable. The quality of air shifts, and the overall vibe of the environment changes. Once the night awakens, there is a brand new symphony of sounds as the nocturnal creatures and insects report for duty. The melodious songs of birds are replaced by the harmonious sounds of crickets. Instead of humming bees, you get The humming bees are replaced by high pitched mosquito whistles in your ear.

Amongst the Ancient Egyptians, the direct relationship between the sleep-wake cycle and the life-death cycle was understood and recorded in great detail. The books Am-Tuat and The Book of Gates are thought to be

Stay woke...

a step-by-step guide for navigating both the unconscious mind, as well as the journey from life into death and death into life. These societies placed great value in the ability to successfully navigate between stages of consciousness.

Once while meditating on this topic, I realized the difference between "falling asleep" and "going to sleep." The first seems to be an involuntary and automatic event wherein the body and mind are overtaken by sleepiness and thus, slips into unconsciousness (sleep). The person that "falls asleep" is often unaware that they are asleep nor that they are dreaming, until they have awakened. And in many cases, they are totally unaware of the exact moment when they actually fell asleep.

Those who "go to sleep" have a completely different experience. These are the people who literally, and with full intention, cross over from the waking state into the realm of sleeping. They slow down their brain activity, and slowly release their grip on consciousness (awakeness) in order to crossover, with full consciousness (awareness) into the world of sleep. The person who is aware of being asleep, while actually sleeping, is said to experience *lucid dreaming*. This is when you are aware that you are dreaming while in the dream, and capable of manipulating your dreams through purposeful direction. This is directly related to the information-retrieval theory of dreaming discussed earlier in this chapter, and is very useful as a cognitive tool.

Some consciousness researchers see lucid dreaming and the ability to maintain conscious awareness, while changing stages of conscious awakeness, as key to maintaining conscious awareness as one transitions from life to death. This seems to be at the core of the Ancient Egyptian notions of an after-life, wherein the recently deceased sought to maintain their awareness as they traveled between "worlds." Some claim this is how they were able

Practical Psychology 101

to provide such a detailed mapping of the Tuat (the Underworld). In the text, the soul of the deceased is shown traveling with their spirit guides and answering certain questions in order to pass through the many gates. This information was to be learned, practiced, and memorized while alive, then utilized by the deceased, once they died. It was a sort of psychological (soul) map.

This understanding is at the root of many systems of initiation; it is also a natural part of the growth process. Again, Ancient Egyptians held this understanding at the core of their philosophy, be it spiritual, educational, political, economical, social, or psychological. As mentioned earlier, one's sense of awareness can be increased even as the levels of awakeness "decrease," even to the point of death.

The Ancient Egyptian philosophy of life was to prepare for death, meaning to live your life as if it will continue *on and on and on and on*, beyond your physical death, in a way that reflects, perfectly, what you do while you are living it. To believe that there is an ultimate end, allows for people to live as if they wont continue to reap from this life; instead, they live recklessly, as if this is the only one.

The Per-t Em Heru are both instructions for living and instructions for traveling on the various levels of awakeness-consciousness: from being wide awake, to literally being "dead." We find in Chapter 125 of the Per-t Em Heru (sometimes called Spell #125) the process of passing through the various gates/levels of the Tuat (Unconscious/Underworld). Contained within this portion are the now famous *"42 Negative Confessions of Maat,"* sometimes called the *"42 Declarations of Maat"* from which the *Ten Commandments* of the *Old Testament* are derived.[23] If in no other place within the Kemetic tradition, we will surely find here, a complex and insightful treatment of the

23   Recall that Moses was an Egyptian Prince and Initiated Priest, having access to all of the Sacred Knowledge and Science of Egypt.

unconscious aspects of human psychology (soul). Beautiful symbolism is used to describe not only how one should approach the shift in awakeness–consciousness from life to death, but also how one should work to maintain awareness–consciousness during this transition known as "death." The depth of this philosophy is rivaled by few things known to this world.

In this one body of work, we find instructions of how one should live their life in order to prepare for the next phase of living. It is believed that this information was literally retrieved by a reconnaissance team of highly-trained priests, who were capable of traveling beyond this veil separating life and death, maintain their awareness-consciousness while doing it, and once again return to the living side of the threshold. As more were trained to function in a similar manner, there became more and more conscious beings (or beings that the living were now more conscious of) on the other side (Ancestors, called Shepsu in the Kemetic language), with whom communication could be established and/or maintained.

This philosophy and science of being able to communicate with one's Ancestors is found around the world, amongst almost every known culture. Even those who are unaware of this fact, are likely participating in rituals that are clear indications of this ability to honor and communicate with Ancestors (funerals, naming of streets, buildings, children, pouring out liquor, etc.).

Again, we ask: Why is knowledge of consciousness important, and what does it have to do with social justice movements? In regards to awareness, it should be obvious. The degree of sensory awareness that a person has, often determines what they are capable of perceiving from their environment. In the case of a social justice rally or protest, awareness can mean the difference between life and death, incarceration or freedom, success and ultimate failure.

Practical Psychology 101

There are often reports of *agent provocateurs* being present at protests and demonstrations, for the sole purpose of disrupting and misdirecting the otherwise focused intentions of the protesters or demonstrators. If one is not aware of the presence of these individuals, they may be more susceptible to their influence and disruptive tactics.

As mentioned in the introduction, I once attended a rally with a colleague in the aftermath of an urban uprising. As we walked around the area, I noticed two young White males standing in the background. Initially, they appeared to be teenage punk rockers, just hanging out, however, upon further observation, it was clear that they were there on some sort of intentional mission. Perhaps my training as a micro-facial expressions and body language interpreter assisted me in identifying them. Maybe it was also my heightened sense of awareness that allowed me to see that one of the "by-standers" was wearing a bulletproof vest under his t-shirt and jacket. I pointed them out to my colleague who hadn't noticed their presence, nor the fact that at least one of them was wearing body-armor.

I decided to walk over and strike up a conversation with them, in order to verify what I had previously perceived. My colleague and I walked over and I greeted the two guys. They returned the greeting, after which I asked about the image on the vest-wearer's t-shirt. He told me it was the image of a young Bill Murray, and after a little more "small talk" I asked if they were working security or something? He responded "Yeah, something like that." So I told him I'd noticed he was wearing a "vest" and that they were obviously on some of mission and stood out to me.

I assured them that most people probably had not noticed the vest, but they should still take care as they did whatever they were here to do. I told them of my work and training, and how this contributed to my ability to identify them as such, even though they were attempting to be undercover. They seemed relieved and bid us farewell as we walked away and they vacated the premises.

I encourage all people to understand and increase the awareness aspect of their consciousness. The more you are able to gather and discern from your sensory awareness, the more access you will gain to information about yourself, your environment and others, on a more efficient and effective basis. You can begin to better understand the mind-state of people around you simply by using subtle body cues. You will have the gift of prediction, being able to know that something will happen before most people are even aware of its possibility.

Sharpening cognitive tools like selective attention, direct inner awareness, and the many aspects of extrasensory perception, will give you a thinking and perceptual advantage over most others who fail to acknowledge, much less intentionally develop, these sometimes latent and dormant abilities.

Understanding and using the awakeness aspect of consciousness can prove equally beneficial by expanding the use of our personal sleep-wake cycle, and the conscious experiencing of the mind. This practice will assist in the retrieval of beneficial information from dreams, understanding the unconscious influencers of our conscious behaviors and experiences, as well as provide you with an expanded sense of self.

Although closely related and easily made to work together, the awake and aware aspects of consciousness are totally independent of each other. This means that one can be totally asleep, and maintain a heightened sense of awareness of what is going on around them;[24] and vice versa. A person can be wide awake and totally oblivious

---

24   Think about the person who is asleep, but wakes up when you turn the tv off claiming they were watching it—you have actually awakened them from a tv-induced trance.

to what is happening right next to them. There are also cases where a person is "sound asleep" and has no idea that someone is trying to wake them up by calling their name or even shaking their leg. Likewise, there are those who are wide awake and totally aware of the most subtle things occurring in the environment.

The beautiful part of consciousness is that it can be trained and strengthened through various exercises and practices. For all those who are involved in social justice movements, it should be a top priority to enhance the consciousness of yourself and your group by exploring these consciousness raising tools, and employing them both through practice, and in real-time on the frontlines. Mastering the various ways of utilizing and manipulating consciousness, makes you an intentional factor when it comes to determining your identity and sense of self. This directly impacts how you perceive what is taking place both within, and around you, and is an important step towards becoming a more efficient and effective social justice activist and organizer.

Chapter 5
On autopilot...

Learning is perhaps one of the most popular, yet highly misunderstood aspects of psychology for non-psychology professionals. I suspect this is due to our tendency to relate learning to the classroom context, or as some form of instruction being given to students, with little reference to it as a psychological tool. Ask anyone about learning and they will almost always refer to academics, a classroom, the school system, etc. If the person happens to be an educator, their frame of reference will almost certainly be a school setting, and the conversation will likely involve thinking and learning styles, and almost inevitably, make mention of students and teachers.

Yes, education does employ tools found in the science of learning, however, it is not the totality of learning; nor is learning the totality of education. They overlap, but are distinguishable from one another. Therefore, in this chapter, we want to take our understanding of learning beyond "education," and see it as a psychological process for influencing thoughts, beliefs, emotions, and behaviors. A process wherein students become the conditioned, and teachers, the conditioners.

According to psychology, willing participation is not a requirement for learning. In fact, a person does not even have to be aware that they are "learning." Ironically, it sometimes works better if they aren't aware. This is fascinating stuff. However, before we get into that analysis, let's "slow walk" our understanding of the concept by first drawing a distinction between knowledge and information, along with a brief discussion of *truth* and its independence from *belief* and *knowing*.

Distinguishing knowledge from information helps us to discern between the knowledgeable and the well-informed. Knowledge is having a command of information, concepts, and is a method of exploring information, while information are bits of data that stand independent of anyone being aware of them. Information is the detail of who, what, when, where, why, and how. It is data. As the word implies, it is the forming of a concept into something concrete and tangible. Because it is data, it is designed to be unintelligibly stored, and recalled and recited without the need for knowledge, understanding, and wisdom.

The word "science" comes from the Latin word "scio, scire, scivi, scitus." This word loosely translates as "to know," and refers directly to a certain degree of thorough examination and expertise, and even to developing an understanding of all that is to be known. The Latin term is thought to derive directly from the Greek "skhizein"[25] which means "to split, rend, cleave." This relates knowledge to the process of discernment; understanding how things differ and are separate from each other. Again, knowledge is different from information; in fact, knowledge contains information, but goes beyond the information. For this reason, I like to compare the relationship between knowledge and information to the relationship between a rectangle and a square; all squares are rectangles, but not all rectangles are squares; all knowledge is information, but not all information is knowledge. Keep this in mind as we go deeper into the concept.

In cognitive psychology, we say something has

---

25   Ironically, this is closely related to the word "schizophrenic," which also relates to the splitting of something; specifically, the mind.

On autopilot...

been "learned" once there is a change in how the individual mentally engages the world. I specify "mentally engages" because there are times where physical injury and/or deficiency may cause a person to physically engage the world differently, which does not necessarily reflect, require or involve learning. Now a person with a non-congenital disability, meaning one who was not born with the "disability," will definitely as a default have to learn how to engage the world with a "disability." A person born with a "disability" is also learning how to engage the world, however, it is the same learning process as one who does not have a "disability," meaning they are learning, as children, how to engage the world, for the first time; an experience much different than an individual losing use of a limb after 75 years of having unhindered access and utility.

Consider this analogy: a librarian at the *Library of Congress* has access to one of the world's greatest repositories of information. In this position, the librarian is knowledgeable about how to access every bit of information; in regards to this information, they are only well-informed. Now if this same librarian has internalized and mastered the information, beyond simple recall, as demonstrated by their ability to apply it to random, varied, and spontaneous situations, they are now exhibiting their possession of knowledge. Concretely, if this same librarian utilizes the methods of organizing the LOC information, at home with their possessions (clothes, books, food, etc.), maximizing storage and retrieval, and providing a high level of efficiency, they are demonstrating knowledge; information has been transferred and applied to a different situation.

Information contributes to some forms of knowledge, while other forms exist beyond the need for, and/or access to, information. These are the direct experiences mentioned by some mystics where they suddenly are aware of knowing something, without knowing how they

Practical Psychology 101

came to know it. Think about the scene in *The Matrix* where Neo, played by Keanu Reaves, is "taught" Kung Fu. He wakes up from his computer-induced "trance" and with surprise and confidence states, "I know Kung Fu." To which Morpheus, played by Laurence Fishburne, replies, "Show me."

What about information and truth? Most people have probably had an experience where they receive information, but it was wrong, meaning, it was not true, and thereby leaving them misinformed. The following sayings are common, but may or may not actually be true. In some cases, we can be more certain about their validity than in others; however, there is room to question them all:

2 + 2 = 4. There are 50 states in the United States of America. There are seven continents. Women are from Venus and Men are from Mars. It is better to always eat your dinner before having dessert. To err is human. Eve came from Adam's rib. Everything in moderation. Pluto is no longer a planet. It's not what you know, but what you can prove. The burden of proof is on you. History is a lie agreed upon.

Some of the above statements can be made to be true or false, while others are more definitive and absolute. The former is demonstrated by the "2 + 2 = 4" equation. This can be true if the "two's" being added are of the same subject, meaning if there are two keys plus two keys, then your total number of keys equals four keys. It can be made false if the "two's" being added are of different subjects. For example, two cars + two giraffes equals two cars and two giraffes, not four "caraffes." It can be made true by further qualifying the equation with more details on the question side of things. If the question is "how many things does a person add to their possessions if they are given two giraffes and two cars?" The correct answer is four; so in this case, 2 + 2 = 4.

I know, I can hear you saying, what does this have

to do with anything? How is this beneficial to my understanding of truth, knowledge and information? The benefit is in the exercise of seeing any and everything (subject, situation, concept, idea, experience, etc.) from as many different angles, perspectives, and through the broadest lens of perception as possible. This is the circumspection ascribed to the Kemetic (Ancient Egyptian) Neteru (deity) Heru (Horus).

Symbolized by the hawk because of the hawk's keen eyesight and the amazing heights that it flies, those who have "awakened" their Heru have the quality of being circumspect and gaining a "bird's eye view" of any situation or thing. This view is what helps us to know about the subject. This places us in the optimal position to use sound judgment when making a decision. It is truly a choice between following what we have learned to be "true," for truth's sake, or following our desires, fears, biases, etc. In other words, we have the responsibility and privilege of choosing between truth and non-truth. Self-mastery is being willing to choose truth even if it brings one pain, loss, or a less pleasurable experience than the other path.

Having a wide context within which to sort and ponder life gives one the advantage of being able to relate to the world. This is true diplomacy. The degree to which one is able to relate, directly translates into emotional intelligence, understanding, and a superior handling of most things. This is so because, as the old adage goes, "nothing has a property in and of itself, it is all about how it relates to other things." Coming into a house that is 79 degrees, from an outside temperature of 95 degrees, makes the inside feel cool. Coming into the same house with a temperature of 79 degrees from an outside temperature of 46 degrees makes the inside feel warm. This is true because the interpretation of how the temperature feels, is directly related to the outside temperature and how it relates to your body temperature. The same is true for the person stepping out of a warm shower in the winter. It's always relative, and therefore subject to perception.

There are times when what you *know*, you actually *know*, but the information may not be *true*. For example, let's say you meet someone and they tell you their name is Michael. You become friends with Michael and 15 years later you are asked to identify the individual by name. Of course you say "Michael" and are suddenly surprised when the detective tells you his real name is Sam, as in Samantha, and that he is actually a she. What you knew, was not true. However, it is knowledge, based on what you have learned. In this case, the information making up your knowledge was false. You have been misinformed.

This section of the manual can be a bit tricky because we are positioning ourselves to think about thinking, and to learn about learning. It is likely that what we think about learning, and what we have learned about thinking, will get in our way at times. Nonetheless, I am confident that by the end of this chapter, we will have a better and more practical knowledge and understanding of the subject, and will see how it relates to social justice movements.

I was once told that sometimes, "what many accept as the truth is no more than a lie agreed upon." And that so much of what we learn today as truthful and factual information, is actually based upon consensus; meaning, a group of people, more or less, agreed that this is what it is; this can be done even with things that are absolutely and sometimes intentionally wrong. Entire paradigms are built in this way. Sure there is some research, experimentation, and true science employed in many cases, however, there are some pretty important questions that are "resolved" simply based on the aforementioned consensus. Let's take Pluto's recent demotion from planetary status. For as long as I have been alive, Pluto was considered a planet.

On autopilot...

In recent years, this has changed. A group of scientists have decided that it will no longer be classified as a planet, based on whatever logic and reasoning they could agree upon, and "poof," it is no more. Another, and perhaps more relevant example is found in the Diagnostic and Statistical Manual of Mental Disorders (DSM). This book houses the classification of mental disorders and is based upon consensus. What may have been considered a mental disorder yesterday, is no longer one today. Some of this is based on progress and an advancement of understanding human psychology, other changes may be more political in nature.

It's important to also understand that people don't always believe what they are promoting as truth. In other words, intentional deception does exist. For example, the best actors in Hollywood strive to convince you that the fictitious character they are portraying, is real: that their every emotion, every thought, action, word, and even their appearance are 100% authentic. The better they are at doing this, the higher their reward (more roles, higher pay, more fame).

Many actors are clear that they are pretending, however, there are those cases where an actor gets so fully into their role that they become enmeshed with the character and begin to adopt certain characteristics into their "real" personality. Tupac Shakur allegedly had this experience while portraying the character "Bishop" in the movie *Juice.*[26] Many hip hop artists, portraying characters for entertainment, often become enmeshed with the character and eventually stay in "mode," which is why many rappers rarely go by their "real" name; instead, they are always addressed by their stage name. On the flip side, when Denzel Washington plays a character, and is interviewed about the movie, they aren't calling him "Malcolm X" or "Memphis

---

26   http://www.mtv.com/news/1677509/rapfix-live-tupac-juice-naughty-by-nature-treach/

Practical Psychology 101

Bleek," he is Denzel Washington. This demonstrates the relationship between personality and learning. In these examples, the actor is rewarded for acting, often deriving pleasure from the role. As with Tupac and other rappers, the reward can be so great that it actually shifts their personality. This is an example of the behaviorist perspective.

Less benign examples of this same phenomenon can be found when medical doctors prescribe certain harmful agents and procedures to their patients that they themselves would never use, or allow to happen to them or their loved ones. The deception is in giving hope that the procedure or medicines will help the patient to get better, and/or that the benefits outweigh the risks. The promotion of the "food pyramid" as a healthy standard for dietary reference and living is another example.

So why are we opening a chapter on learning with this discussion? Simply because what you "learn" and how you learned it, will shape your understanding and experience of reality, which also determines how you interact with the environment around you. In the case of "front-line," social justice movements, people decide whether or not to join, as well as in what capacity they will participate, based on what they believe and have been informed about the situation at hand. The discussion and protests inspired by Colin Kaepernick, formerly of the San Francisco 49ers, is a perfect example of this phenomenon.

Some are all for Kaepernick's decision to protest injustice and police brutality by refusing to stand for the *National Anthem.* In fact, some have themselves decided to boycott all NFL related activities, including watching and attending games, until Colin is hired by a team. Others, who understand the dangers of playing football, specifically in light of the recent discovery of the relationship between concussions, degenerative brain disease (CTE), and playing football, see this as a blessing in disguise and

On autopilot...

would rather Mr. Kaepernick not return to the game, for the sake of his health.

There seems to be this rigid dividing line between those who support this form of protest and those who do not. Those who support the protest may negatively criticize those who decide to continue standing for the *National Anthem*, while those who do not support the protest, consider the gesture to be disrespectful, ineffective, and maybe even futile. Then there are those who support Kaepernick's right to protest, but have decided that they themselves will not participate. Some in the above categories are operating based on *operant conditioning*. Meaning they are choosing to participate, or not, based on the potential and/or actual experience of *reward* and *punishment* for their behaviors.

Some celebrities have openly spoken against Mr. Kaepernick. Some speak out of fear of punishment for associating with Kaepernick, while others speak out against him, perhaps, because they are receiving, or hoping to receive, a reward for doing so. A recent example is Michael Vick, who spoke out against Kaepernick, and was soon after given a talk show. We cannot say for sure that his new show is a direct result of his speaking against Kaepernick, however, the proximity of the incidents makes it a good bet that it is definitely a coincidence (coinciding incident, not happenstance).

On his latest album, *Boomiverse*, Big Boi (one half of the "Mighty Outkast") mentions how people cheered for Kaepernick when he was throwing the ball, but when he decided to take a knee, all that changed. Lost in all of this is Kaepernick's original reason for protesting: not against the flag, nor America, nor the *National Anthem*, but against police brutality and the "justified" killings of unarmed American Africans.

On the flip-side, there may be those who are participating in a similar style of protest simply because they want to be rewarded by news coverage, photo ops, and social media attention. This form of participation is viewed by some to be less genuine and even superficial, I am not here to judge that, I am simply pointing out that there are many motivating forces behind individual decisions to protest; and these forces matter, just like Black lives. We will return to our discussion about operant conditioning later, for now, let us look further into the difference between information and knowledge.

Remember, acquiring information is not the same as obtaining knowledge. Being informed is having one's thought process shaped by facts and details about a particular subject. The information may or may not be true, and the way it is collected and used to form an opinion or thought, or even how it guides the thinking process may or may not lead to actual knowledge. On the other hand, knowledge is having a command of information regarding a situation, person, place or thing.

According to Dictionary.com:

> Information applies to facts told, read, or communicated that may be unorganized or even unrelated...
> Knowledge is an organized body of information, or the comprehension and understanding consequent on having acquired and organized a body of facts.

Based on these definitions, there is a world of difference between knowledge and information. For one, knowledge involves a certain level of understanding, which itself, provides for a degree of flexibility of thought, comprehension, and implementation of that which was acquired. Information, on the other hand is simply anything as basic as a sound overheard from a distance; no connection, insight, or even a thought is necessary, just the act of experiencing the sound provides information. Looked at another way, information is like the raw materials used

On autopilot...

to build a house, all thrown into a pile, or each in their respective places in the hardware store; knowledge is this same material, constructed into a home based on a blueprint or architect's plans.

There is a scene in the movie *Limitless*, where the main character ingests a brain-enhancement drug for the first time. He encounters his landlord's wife in the hallway on his way to his apartment. She begins to argue with him, and as she does so, the pill kicks in, and his internal dialogue becomes audible to the viewer. He narrates how the stored and formerly "useless" and disjointed information (things he has seen while watching T.V., or heard in passing, a book he may have glimpsed while walking past the front window of a bookstore, etc.) is now being assembled into organized and useful knowledge, which then allowed him to become knowledgeable regarding just about anything, including the subject matter of the paper his landlord's wife was writing for law school. He was also simultaneously becoming more perceptive of the things he was sensing. This shows the relationship between sensation, perception, and knowledge. You'll have to see the movie to learn of his reward for demonstrating this knowledge.

Before the pill, he had information. After the pill, he had knowledge and was knowledgeable. The difference between the two conditions was more vast than night and day, it was more like the difference we perceive between the ocean floor and deep space (which actually may not be that different...maybe we will find out one day). Unfortunately, in today's culture, the informed are exalted and praised for having information, regardless of their inability to assemble that data into a well organized and functional body of knowledge, useful and necessary for their own personal evolution and refinement. Knowing has its reward too, in fact, it is its own reward.

Those interested in forming or participating in

Practical Psychology 101

social justice movements such as *Black Lives Matter*, will greatly benefit from this perspective of "learning." The key to this is understanding that there is a difference between being informed and being knowledgeable. An informed protester may have the facts about the issues at hand, and how previous protests have played out; a knowledgeable protester will likely not be a protester at all, but will be an organizer, one who has strategized and has clearly defined goals for being involved in the "movement" in a very intentional, and deliberate way.

The informed protester is led throughout the city on predetermined routes, determined by law enforcement as a means of containing the protesters and minimizing the dangers of property damage and injured people. All without realizing they are being "herded" and managed.[27] The knowledgeable protester realizes this ahead of time and makes a conscious decision to participate or not; understanding both the benefits and consequences of such actions. The informed protester is more likely to function off of pure emotion and adrenaline, while the knowledgeable protester may maintain use of what cognitive psychologist refer to as *executive cognitive functioning* or *higher-order thinking*. These are tools like reasoning, deep analytical and synthesis-based thinking, comprehension, organization of sensory perception, enhanced spatial reasoning and situational awareness, along with various other functions designed to enhance and preserve life by preventing and avoiding danger.

It is also important for us to understand that there are many ways of acquiring knowledge; in other words, there are multiple ways of knowing. Some have to study and perform various mental exercises in order to convert

27   I actually recognized this while watching an aerial view of a protest on the news. Certain streets were blocked off, and law enforcement officers were lining the streets ushering the people along the predetermined route.

94

On autopilot...

information into knowledge, while others can awaken from a dream with newly acquired knowledge. Some can be exposed to a small bit of information and through the use of analogy, develop the necessary understanding to claim and demonstrate knowledge of the subject.

This is why highly intelligent people can drop out of elementary school and still be amongst the most knowledgeable people on the planet; and equally how a person who has gone through 12 years of school, college, graduate school and professional school, can still be an idiot; with very little knowledge but tons of information. This is the medical doctor working at a cancer center who takes smoke breaks. Well informed, but has not the ability to change the information into functional knowledge that refines their own behavior.

Let's use the following dialogue to further illustrate our point:

Clerk: Sir, your flight has been delayed.

Man: I know.

Clerk: How did you know that?

Man: I was informed by that lady over there.

As seen in the above example, information can lead to knowledge, but simply having the information does not guarantee knowledge, as illustrated by the following example:

Man: I have read fifteen books on how to fix a car...they were all quite informative, and were written by the leading experts in the field.

Woman: So can you help me to fix my car? It seems to be a minor problem with the brake lights.

Man: I remember reading all about brake lights, and feel that I am well informed, but I am afraid I do not know how to fix one.

Woman: Ok. I guess I'd better find someone who knows what they are doing.

Practical Psychology 101

In fact, my sister has done it before, I am sure she knows how.

Man: Did she go to school to learn how to work on cars? Or did she read a lot of books on the subject?

Woman: No. She was always very inquisitive as a child...she's the type that dives right in and figures things out by herself. She has gained a lot of knowledge in this way.

And yet, there are other ways that one becomes knowledgeable, which are not so popular and definitely not so readily accepted by the mainstream. In our chapter on consciousness, we explored the various aspects of dreaming, and why we do it. One of the reasons discussed is acknowledged and maintained by many indigenous cultures around the world; that is, the use of dreams as a tool for communicating, learning and gathering information.

It is an old-school, underground tradition, held amongst American Africans in the south, that dreams can provide you valuable information. Some use symbols in their dreams to determine which lottery numbers to pick; others use dream symbols to determine how to deal with certain situations. Time and time again I have heard stories of how a grandmother dreamed of fish and KNEW that someone in her family was pregnant. Without fail, she would place a phone call and confirm what she had learned from her dream. This particular example highlights another phenomenon known as *archetypes* and the *collective unconscious.* Briefly, archetypes are a set of symbols that are known to represent the same or similar concepts, to many people, who are ordinarily separated by distance (different continents with no known contact), separated by time (thousands of years), and/or separated by culture (speaking different languages, etc.).

The fact that fish are simultaneously associated with pregnancy by southern grandmothers, by Ancient Egyptians seen in the symbolism associated with the

On autopilot...

Neter Auset/Isis (ocean, fish, pregnancy, nurturing, etc.), and amongst West Africans in Nigeria in the symbolism related to the Orisha Yemaya and Olokun (and in some areas Mami Wata), and a known fertility food, illustrates how knowledge can be gained without seemingly tangible couriers.

It is theorized that these archetypes are stored in an unconscious realm that everyone on the planet can access. This typically occurs beneath the threshold of consciousness, and thus is usually not intentionally attempted. However, there are those who participate in *lucid dreaming*, where they "go to sleep" rather than "fall asleep," thereby maintaining conscious awareness while they are sleeping and dreaming (the average person only realizes they were asleep once they have awakened). There are hundreds of dream books on the shelves of bookstores and online, some of which are designed to focus on the relationship between dream symbolism and numbers, others identifying specific animals in dreams and lending an interpretation of what the symbol means to the life of the dreamer, while others focus on the theory behind dreaming.

As mentioned earlier in this chapter, information consists of bits of data or facts, not necessarily organized. I gave the example of how every bit of stimulation, every thought, every experience provides information for you. In the case of dreams, every person, sound, sight, smell, experience, sensation, word, color, pattern, movement, interaction, relationship, activity, the method used to do things, literally everything in the dream is a bit of information. From a typical perspective, dreams are just dreams: some weird, some crazy, some scary, some erotic, but all just dreams with no meaning or correlation to the externalized, "real world." However, if one understands how to interpret the information provided by dreams (as instructed by the dream books, and ancient methods mentioned earlier), they may be capable of organizing the information and thereby gaining knowledge from their dreams. Psychiatrists Sigmund Freud and Carl Jung, as well as an unknown number of indigenous people have used dreams in this manner.

To summarize this section on the distinction between knowledge and information, it is important for us to look closely at the definitions provided earlier. The distinction is in the organization of facts and data (information) in order to develop an understanding (knowledge). Remember, a librarian has access to all kinds of information by virtue of the fact that they are custodians of books; yet, this does not automatically grant them knowledge of what is inside the books. For that, they would have to, in one way or another, gather the information in the books, then organize that information in such a way that they are capable of comprehending the subject, and by some means, demonstrate their competency.

Knowledge and information are obtained in a variety of ways. Some methods are more reliable and held in higher esteem than others; this depends heavily on the worldview of the beholder. As with many aspects of culture, individuals have their own unique learning styles and thus, tend to gravitate towards those subjects and experiences that are most in-line with their intellectual disposition. Too often, there is an over emphasis on left-brain-based learning and teaching styles, while those of the right-brain or dual-hemispheric orientations are left to sink or swim. Regardless of learning styles and preferences, behavior psychologists have developed methods for "teaching" people and animals to modify their behavior, with very little conscious intention on the part of the learner. This is the intriguing world of *operant* and *classical conditioning* (more on these later).

As mentioned earlier, of all the areas of psychology

On autopilot...

that deal specifically with learning, cognitive psychologists may have the most complex definition and conceptualization of learning. To them, learning is the process through which an organism makes a relatively permanent change in the way they mentally represent the environment based on practice and/or experiences. These mental changes may influence behavior, but may not determine it in full.

This understanding of learning gives a great deal of agency to the learner. It allows room for their behavior to be influenced by their own free will; meaning, a person can gain information that then shapes their understanding of, and relationship to dogs, but they can still act against what they have learned. Let's say their perspective is that dogs are nasty because they like to lick things. Regardless of this mental representation of dogs, a person can still bring themselves to pet a dog without being repulsed by their tongues lapping away at their outstretched hand.

As with most things, this approach to learning may be more beneficial to some than to others. It may facilitate learning in some situations and be totally useless in others. Some consider this to be the more humane approach to learning, and therefore prefer it to the more forceful and sometimes non-consensual methods employed by behaviorists.

According to behavior psychologists, learning is a relatively permanent change in behavior as a result of practice and/or experience. These changes can occur on an unconscious level, meaning a person or organism can be taught certain behaviors, with or without knowing they are learning. Along these lines, behaviors can be modified in very subtle and sometimes insidious ways. This definition orients behavior as the key element for measuring if an individual has actually learned. Therefore, the observable physical manifestations of the internal processes (thinking, emotions, etc.) are seen as some of the few, truly measurable, indications of what a person knows, how they feel, and perhaps even what they are thinking. This is so because behaviorists tend to rely on methods that bypass, or at least minimizes the use of the conscious aspects of cognition. In other words, a behaviorist modifies behavior by subtle and repeated associations, and can do so, again, whether or not the subject is aware of what is taking place.[28] We cannot stress this point enough.

Again, there are two main vehicles by which behavior-based learning takes place: operant conditioning and classical conditioning. These will be the focus of this section. The first, and perhaps more complex form of conditioning for consideration is classical. This is where a "neutral" or unrelated stimulus is used to generate a response that something else naturally generates. This is done by pairing the *neutral stimulus* with the one that usually creates the response. In technical terms, the stimulus that naturally creates the response is called the *unconditioned stimulus* (*US*), and the natural response that is evoked by the *US* is called the *unconditioned response* (*UR*). Once the neutral stimulus is capable of generating the unconditioned response (UR), after repeated instances of pairing with the unconditioned stimulus (US), then it goes from being a "neutral" stimulus to a *conditioned stimulus* (*CS*), and the unconditioned response (UR) is now considered to be a *conditioned response* (*CR*), although it is the exact same response as the previous unconditioned response (UR).

All those Us, Rs, and Cs can seem confusing so let me further illustrate by detailing the experiments that brought on knowledge of this form of conditioning. The first is Ivan Pavlov and his salivating dog. In the 1920s, Ivan Pavlov was experimenting on dogs. His purpose was to identify neural receptors (nerve endings) in a dog's mouth that were responsible for triggering salivation. In

On autopilot...

order to measure the salivation, tubes were connected to the salivary glands from the outside of the dog's mouth, making the saliva filling the tubes visible. The experimenters placed meat powder on the tongue of the dogs in order to initiate salivation. As the experiment went on, the dogs began to salivate at "odd" times. For example, as the lab assistants walked into the room, the dogs would salivate; and even if the researchers simply and unintentionally banged metal trays together it would illicit salivation.

At first, these incidents were viewed as problematic because the salivation was occurring off schedule. They later realized they were on to something big. Upon further exploration, Pavlov realized the dogs had developed a sense of anticipation for the meat powder, associating the events that preceded the powder on their tongue, with the actual powder being placed on their tongues. He then set out to scientifically investigate how two unrelated experiences, could be brought together to then produce the same results. He eventually taught the dogs to salivate when they heard a particular tone, or when they saw a particular light turn on.

In this example, the banging of trays, the lab assistant entering the room and other things leading up to the dog's receiving meat powder are all considered "*neutral stimuli*," in the first part of the experiment. The meat powder is an *unconditioned stimulus* (*US*) because it naturally produces salivation in the dogs, which in relation to the meat powder, is an *unconditioned response* (*UR*). Once the sound of the trays, the presence of the lab assistants, etc., began producing salivation, they became the *conditioned stimuli* (*CS*), and the resulting salivation, a *conditioned response* (*CR*).

From the behaviorist perspective, this learning was automatic and involuntary, meaning it would occur whether or not the subject was aware of the intentions and whether or not they wanted to learn the behavior. On the contrary, cognitive theorist place the emphasis on the information gained by the experience and the mental association between the events producing the outcomes. Yes, in both cases, there is an unconscious mental association that takes place, however, from the cognitive perspective, it does not necessarily translate into an observable change in behavior.

How does this impact our day-to-day lives? Are there instances where there is an involuntary pairing of two unrelated things to produce the same results? The short answer is absolutely. The longer answer follows.

In my last book, *Symbolically Speaking, Vol. 1*, I briefly spoke about the association of hip hop music with violence and negative experiences in movies.

> "It's the reason why in movies, the music often shifts to some sort of 'hip hop-ish' beat when the scene switches to a 'dangerous' or otherwise 'urban' environment. It sets the tone for how you will feel watching that scene, and in similar environments in real life." (p. 46)

Without mentioning the actual words "classical conditioning," I was surely referring to the scientific process. This association has far reaching implications and is perhaps directly related to the recent barrage of unarmed (and even legally armed) American African children, men and women being shot and killed by law enforcement. Is it possible that the targets, typically used at gun ranges, when coupled with various other forms of propaganda, condition police officers to shoot at "Black" people? Granted there is a large variety of targets used at gun ranges these days, the standard version is typically a black, "male" silhouette.

In a recent episode of the television series *Atlanta*, there was a scene where an American African male character, Darius, who is played by Lakeith Stanfield, went to

On autopilot...

a gun range with a paper target featuring a canine. The White male shooters at the range were upset by his choice of target and actually confronted him. In the dialogue that followed, prior to Darius being removed from the range at gunpoint, the White males expressed how upset their kids would be if they were there, simply because he was shooting at a piece of paper with a dog on it. Why? Because, "You can't shoot dogs!" exclaimed one of the White males.

Darius responded with an articulated confusion about how these men were okay with shooting human targets, but upset by a dog target. He also pointed out how the dogs in his neighborhood are crazy; "they bite babies." This illustration shows how a paper target can, and often does, represent what the real life targets, and perceived threats are, or will eventually become. Remember, this is usually involuntary learning, but can be, and often is, related to a real life experience.

When news programs overly focus on reporting crimes where the suspects are American Africans, and show the image of the alleged perpetrator, in association with the story about the crime, viewers stand the chance of becoming conditioned to associate criminal behaviors with those who are most closely related to the images being shown. The race of a suspect is almost predictable when there is no image being shown. Many would bet they are White, and would likely be correct.

A current example is found with the teen suspects who were seen striking and throwing matches in East Tennessee, allegedly leading to the dramatic fires of Gatlinburg in 2016. Their images were never shown and they were actually released from custody, although there were witnesses. Media sources cited the state law that prevents images of minors from being shown unless they are being tried as adults. Meanwhile in Nashville, also in Tennessee, American African male teenagers were charged with a crime, around the same time, and were also being held as minors, yet their images were shown on the news and in the newspapers.

I shared the article via social media and someone actually claimed to recognize one of the American African males as the person that attempted to rob her at gunpoint while walking to her car after work. Now whether it was him or not, by posting these images, it potentially makes all young Black males suspect. It may also be the reason why cops claim to "fear for their lives," when they aggressively confront American African males.

The use of classical conditioning to generate certain emotional responses was investigated by Dr. John Watson and Rosalie Rayner in their famous experiments with "Little Albert." Using a rabbit, they demonstrated how humans can be conditioned to become fearful of ordinarily and previously non-scary things, simply by associating these non-scary things with something that actually produces fear and/or a startle response. A detailed discussion on emotions is found in the next chapter, suffice it to

On autopilot...

say, for now, our emotional state impacts our behavior and even our cognitive processes. Neuroscientists have identified the negative impact of highly emotional states on the executive cognitive functioning of the brain. This is why soldiers are systematically conditioned out of their natural emotional and physiological responses to potential dangers and fear invoking situations like gun fire, explosions, and other forms of life threatening violence.

Drs. Pavlov and Watson were capable of intentionally manipulating the pairing of stimuli and response, in order to produce desired and predictable results. This has been demonstrated time and time again by various researchers and everyday people. It's not a difficult process, and does not necessarily require any advance training to pull off. Martin Seligman, in the mid-1970s, conducted another set of experiments demonstrating conditioning's ability to alter behaviors.

In his research, Seligman associated the ringing of a bell with the administration of electric shock to dogs. In his initial experiments, he observed how, after pairing the bell with the shock, dogs would react to the bell as if they were being shocked, when no shock had actually been administered. He later took these conditioned dogs and placed them in an area where they were shocked by the floor, with no chance of escaping the shock. The dogs "accepted" their fate and did not continue to seek a way out. In another phase of the experiment, these conditioned dogs were given a way to escape the shock. Instead of removing themselves from the "shock zone," the dogs remained in place and continued to endure the shocks. When dogs, who were not conditioned by the shocks, were placed in this same situation (with a way out), they would simply remove themselves from the "shock zone" by jumping over the barrier.

This is where the concepts of *learned helplessness*

and *learned hopelessness* originate. The dogs, through conditioning, learned that they were helpless to improve their situation, so they simply and literally laid down in defeat, even when a way out was provided for them. Other researchers have demonstrated this with a hungry fish who was blocked from accessing smaller fish that it would normally eat. A transparent barrier was placed between the predator fish and its prey making them inaccessible. The predator, attempting to access the prey, would run into the barrier and receive the unpleasant sensation of hitting the glass. Once the barrier was removed and the prey fish began swimming freely throughout the aquarium, even in close proximity to the predator fish, the predator would not attempt to capture and eat them. Instead, it would starve, sometimes even to death.

This form of pairing and association of unrelated stimuli and responses is not the only way that conditioning takes place. In addition to classical conditioning, scientist have also identified the use of *rewards* and *punishments* (*reinforcers*) as powerful tools for modifying behavior. This form of learning, called *operant conditioning*, is closely related to classical conditioning and is often theorized to take place in the same experiments. For example, Little Albert's later avoidance of white fluffy things is thought to be an indication of operant conditioning. His avoiding the objects in a voluntary manner was interpreted to mean that he had learned the relationship between doing or avoiding specific things based on the consequence, which is, by definition, operant conditioning.[29]

It is known that healthy humans will usually gravitate towards pleasure and retract from, and/or avoid pain and punishment. With this being the case, pleasure and

---

29   A form of learning by which an organism learns to participate in certain behaviors (engaging or avoiding) based on the effects (pleasant or unpleasant; desirable or undesirable) of those behaviors.

On autopilot...

reward are used to increase the likelihood of a behavior occurring, while pain and punishment are used to decrease the likelihood of those behaviors occurring. Within the context of operant conditioning, anything that increases the likelihood of a behavior occurring is considered to be a *reinforcer*. Whether you are giving something desirable to the organism (*positive reinforcement*) or removing something undesirable away from the organism (*negative reinforcement*) in order to increase a particular behavior, you are dealing with a reinforcer.

In the world of reinforcers, there are both primary and secondary types. *Primary reinforcers* are things that lead directly to the survival of an organism. Basic needs like nutritional sustenance (food, water), shelter, security, and the avoidance of things that hinder these basic needs are all classified as primary reinforcers. *Secondary reinforcers* are typically those things that help you to secure a primary reinforcer. Money is perhaps the most popular example of secondary reinforcers in the Western world. In its role as a secondary reinforcer, money is used to exchange for many primary reinforcers, however, it cannot itself, serve as food, shelter and security. The stronger the relationship a secondary reinforcer has to a primary reinforcer, the more powerful the effect and utility it will have as a reinforcer.

It's important to remember that secondary reinforcers do not, themselves, directly fulfill basic needs; but are a catalyst for acquiring the things that will fulfill basic needs. An interesting phenomenon often occurs where an individual will forgo a primary reinforcer (food, clothing, shelter) and instead seek a secondary reinforcer (money, social status, fame). I most often experience this when someone on the street is asking for money to buy food and I offer to buy them the food instead. Rather than accepting my offer to buy them food, they'd rather have the money.

Practical Psychology 101

In some cases this is a matter of strategy, where the person, if given the money, can get a little food and use the change to buy something else (bus token, etc.).

However, in many instances, people seek money for the sake of money, fame for the sake of fame, and social status for the sake of social status, while neglecting their pursuit of making basic needs easier to satisfy, although the acquisition of large amounts of money, wealth, fame, and social status can definitely ease the way to meeting basic needs; wealthy people typically don't starve, aren't homeless, and have their choice of comforts. Again, it's true that having money, fame, and social status can make meeting your basic needs easier: famous people often get discounts and free products; wealthy people can invest their money to make more money while spending smaller amounts on meeting their basic needs, etc., but the money itself does not meet the need, it is a tool for meeting the need.

Because humans are social creatures, the secondary reinforcer of social status has been strongly associated with a sense of security, which serves as a primary reinforcer. This can be related by understanding why animals move in herds and how the animal with the highest status in that particular society, is often the one most well taken care of by the rest of the group. As a result of people pursuing secondary reinforcers, such as social status, in place of primary reinforcers, many people are easily influenced to pursue social status, as if it were a primary reinforcer, and behave in ways that may require them to compromise sound judgment and even their moral convictions. This is evidenced by the child who succumbs to peer pressure at school. They can be manipulated into forsaking their own sense of safety and/or morality, in order to fulfill the need to feel socially accepted by a particular group of kids. This can lead to many negative outcomes.

A few years ago, I conducted a small experiment

On autopilot...

as an illustration to my Introduction to Psychology class. The purpose of the experiment was to demonstrate how social pressure and the need to "fit in" plays out in real world settings. I waited until the majority of students had arrived to class, then I instructed them to all agree with me no matter what I said. I stated, "I will draw a circle on the board and call it a triangle. I will ask questions about this 'triangle' and want you all to answer as if the circle really is a triangle."

When the next student walked in, I began class as usual with a review of the material covered in the previous meeting. I then moved forward with the lesson on social psychology, leading with the experiment. As I drew the circle I spoke about triangles and how they all have 3 sides. I asked a student to tell me which of the three sides was longer. The students went along with the experiment. I then called on the unsuspecting student who came in late. I asked him to tell me which angle was the largest. He looked perplexed, chuckled, then began to look around the room to see if anyone else realized there was not a triangle on the board. He finally stated, "Dr. Menzise, that's a circle on the board." I challenged him by retorting that it was in fact a triangle. I then moved on to another student who agreed with me and pointed to a fictitious angle as the largest angle.

I then switched up the experiment to deal with the color of my shirt. In reality it was white, but I called it blue. I then asked the class which blue was darker, my pants or my shirt? The class had various opinions some saying my shirt, others saying my pants, however the late student sat quietly looking confused. I called on him again to give his opinion and he said my shirt was clearly darker. He said it with great conviction, to which the class erupted in laughter. When asked why he decided to go along with his classmates, he said because there was no way that everyone else was wrong and he was right. He figured he was just having a bad day and didn't want it to get worse by seeming to be crazy in a classroom with over 70 of his peers.

There have been many, more sophisticated, examples of how the need to belong socially, impacts a person's thoughts, speech, and actions. The above example was an oversimplified way of showing how the secondary reinforcer of social acceptance and belonging, can trump one's trust in their own ability to correctly sense and perceive the environment, and the reality of their immediate surroundings. It's commonly called peer pressure. There use to be after-school specials for this sort of thing.

This little experiment also demonstrates how a person will avoid punishment by sometimes pretending to believe or by actually believing something that, based on all available evidence (including seeing things with their own eyes) could not be the case. How does this play out in the "real world?" I'm glad you asked. Everyday we are bombarded with examples of how *group-think* overcomes individual thinking. Some argue that, in the situation of group-think, there is very little thinking taking place at all, but instead, the group is led by blind conviction, emotion, and knee-jerk reactions. In situations of group-think, the reward that reinforces the behavior is usually a sense of solidarity and the pleasure of being able to vent frustrations and anger; in other words, sometimes group-think serves as a *catharsis* for people suppressing their frustrations. People also enjoy the protection of anonymity, which decreases the likelihood of being punished.

Keep a group of individuals powerless and frustrated long enough, and they will become hypersensitive to subtle triggers, and more susceptible to being steered towards certain modes of expression, whether to their benefit or detriment. In an episode of *Scandal*, this was

On autopilot...

demonstrated by what was referred to as *"dog-whistle politics."* This is when certain catch phrases and terms are used to trigger only certain segments of the population while others are totally unaware of the trigger having been employed; the name of this phenomenon refers to how only dogs hear dog whistles, while humans do not.

An example of reinforcement being used in a negative sense, meaning something undesired is taken away in order to increase the likelihood of a behavior occurring, is found in the story of a child and their chores. Most children dislike having to complete household chores. For this example we will focus on the child who hates to wash dishes, yet they have to do it three nights each week. The child's parent sets up an agreement where the child will have to do the dishes one less time, per week, for each good report they receive from their teacher at school. The removed, undesired action, is the washing of dishes, the behavior being increased as a result are those things that foster a good report coming from their teacher.

This can also be done with sports teams. Let's say a basketball team typically has to run 30 laps around the track in their daily practice. The coach can strike a deal that for every free throw basket made in a game, 5 laps will be removed from the next practice. This will likely increase the amount of focus and practice given towards making free throw baskets, which in turn may increase the number of shots made during the actual game.

A recent example of how reward and punishment are employed in a real life situation follows. Once again we find ourselves going to Tennessee, The Volunteer State, for our example. A judge recently offered inmates reduced sentences for agreeing to be neutered; yes, literally sterilized. The removal of time from their sentences is considered the reward (negative reinforcer), the behavior being rewarded is their compliance; in this instance, with sterilization.

This example brings up a very important aspect of conditioning that should be explored if we are to get a good understanding of its efficiency and effectiveness for impacting large populations. A person does not have to be the direct recipient of the reward or punishment for their behaviors to be modified in a direction similar to the one receiving the reward or punishment. In the case of the Tennessee inmates, other inmates who see their co-prisoners receiving the reward of a reduced sentence, are more likely to seek out and participate in the same opportunity.

This is the exact same process described in the *"Willie Lynch Letter: How to Make a Slave,"* specifically the part where the author describes taking the strongest male enslaved African, and brutally tarring, feathering, and ripping him in half using horses running in opposite directions; all of this in front of those who respected and saw him as an example of strength and hope. By doing this, the remaining enslaved Africans associated being strong with the threat of physical harm and death, and the source of the heinous punishment they'd just witnessed. This experience is thought to have eventually led to mothers raising their sons to be "weak" and non-threatening, and men to adopt the same characteristics for themselves.

This is eerily similar to how police officers are currently being rewarded for murdering unarmed American Africans, and the subsequent conversations had by mothers who now fear for their son's safety as they leave the house. Sons are often advised, rightfully so, to refrain from doing anything that will make them appear threatening; they are told to be nice, comply, and "don't give them a reason to kill you." Unfortunately, as mentioned earlier, sometimes the "reason" is their skin color, which is not an easy thing to change. On the other hand, the officers are being conditioned to more likely repeat the behavior

On autopilot...

of killing unarmed American Africans because their colleagues are rewarded with paid leave, transfers to other departments, financial buy outs, honored retirements after the wrongful murder, and even by funds being raised for the officer by support groups.

Awareness of conditioning is the first step to reduce one's susceptibility to being conditioned against their will. By paying attention to your own behaviors, thoughts, feelings, etc., and by constantly asking "why" these things occur the way they do, and why they are even occurring in the first place, brings your analytical mind to the forefront of consciousness, creating a situation of introspection and self-analysis. In the case of front-line movements, this skill and habit can mean the difference between life and death, success and failure, incarceration and freedom.

As mentioned in the chapter on emotion, the court jester is perhaps the most powerful person in the King's court because they control and manipulate the emotions of those in the room. The unsuspecting demonstrator, lacking in emotional control, is more likely to be persuaded by circumstances to do things that may lead them down a path they did not intend on journeying, and would have consciously chosen against if given a chance, without this form of training and refinement.

The ability to function in a detached manner is of great importance for this concept to become a reality. The individual that can consciously and intentionally separate their feelings from their thinking from their doing (the ABC of affect, behavior, and cognition), is given an opportunity to exercise choice in their mental, emotional, and behavioral responses to situations, while the person who does not separate, is likely to engage in a knee-jerk reaction, which could be dangerous or otherwise detrimental.

In a recent episode of *Power*, James St. Patrick, played by Omari Hardwick, is advised by his legal counsel to curb his emotional reactions, else he may be perceived as the stereotypically "angry Black male," which would work against him in the long run. Later in the episode, his defense counsel has a high ranking officer on the stand while in court. His defense purposely worked to trigger the emotions of the detective in order to get him to present as angry, volatile, and emotionally undisciplined, in order to weaken his credibility as an officer with integrity.

Understanding which triggers, or stimuli, work to elicit certain and specific responses in others, is what gives an individual the advantage of controlling others, their behaviors and their mode of functioning. A more powerful use for this tool is seeking to understand the things that trigger you, and what your responses are to those triggers, in order that you may be able to control your own behaviors, emotions, and thoughts, and not leave it to others.

This is what Dr. Martin Luther King, Jr. and his followers were demonstrating during their non-violent protests and forms of passive resistance. They underwent training designed to separate their emotional reactions to external situations from their actual behaviors in response to the same. This allowed them to maintain the behaviors of their own choosing. They understood the tactics of provocation; they understood the number one defense against being unwillingly provoked is to control your own response to stimuli, whether it be an unconditioned or a conditioned one. The person capable of not being afraid in the face of a life threatening situation, is the person who retains their higher levels of thinking, reasoning, and problem solving skills, and thereby, maintaining the advantage; or at least they resist being placed at a disadvantage based on emotional manipulation.

The Muslim, male, Somali police officer that shot and killed the White, Australian, woman in Minneapolis is viewed less favorably than the Christian, White, male and

On autopilot...

female officers who kill American African citizens. This is demonstrated by the stories being reported on the situations, and how each individual is portrayed. For example, an unarmed American African victim will often have their "past" brought up as the reporter attempts to subtly justify the shooting, while White criminals who commit mass murders, are often given excuses of being bullied, or having a mental health issue. Some of these discrepancies are referred to as implicit bias, meaning they occur unconsciously, while others are clearly building the concepts and contexts within which conditioning can easily take place.

By decreasing your susceptibility to being conditioned, you are also increasing your power as a self-determining citizen. This keeps you in control of the one thing that you are guaranteed the ability to be in control of, your own person. To forsake this understanding and eventual mastery, is to forfeit this God-given right, and to willingly subject yourself to the will and desires of others. This condition is a true liability, potentially hindering the likelihood of success for social justice movements.

Understanding the value of learning, and how conditioning can and does impact our thoughts, beliefs, behaviors, and emotions is of great importance. Those who are participating in social justice movements should maintain an awareness that there are some elements intentionally designed to influence your understanding and reaction to situations. Be ever aware and vigilant to maintain your ability to choose freely for yourself, regardless of the promise of reward and/or the threat of punishment.

Chapter 6
In your feelings...

We are all, to one degree or another, familiar with emotions. We have all definitely experienced them. It is considered "healthy" for humans to go through a range of emotions, multiple times each and every day. These emotional experiences are a result of both internal and external factors. They can be brought about by a memory, a movie, a TV show, music, a commercial, the presence of a loved one, the presence of an enemy, a smell, a sound, a taste, a thought, the perceived meaning behind someone's words, hormones, etc. While we are well versed in the experiencing of emotions, I'd dare to say that many of us are clueless when it comes to actually understanding emotions, and even more lost when it comes to mastery.

During one of my spiritual initiations, I was taught that: *Emotions Make Poor Leaders But Great Servants.* We were tasked with realizing what neuroscience has later confirmed in regards to the relationship between high emotional states and executive cognitive functioning (higher order thinking): that increased emotions decrease lucidity of cognition; in other words, when experiencing intense emotional states, the pre-frontal cortex of the brain does not function optimally, which in turn impairs decision making, impulse control, analytical thinking, reasoning, and many other important cognitive processes.[30] Intense

https://www.beyondbooksmart.com/executive-function-ing-strategies-blog/emotional-regulation-and-executive-func-

Practical Psychology 101

emotions can also impair sensation and perception, causing people to misinterpret what they are sensing or to perceive something that has not been sensed (see something that isn't there, hear things that haven't made a sound; hallucinations and delusions), and vice versa.

Think back to a time when you were angry, very sad, or otherwise emotionally involved. Try to recall your thoughts during the peak of those emotions. It's likely that you cannot remember what was going through your mind. If you are able to remember, you are likely to recall a looped expression such as "I can't believe this. I can't believe this. I can't believe this..." Or maybe even some visual imaginings of what you wanted to do, or wish was done, in response to whatever triggered your emotions; like the visual of physically assaulting someone or engaging your "crush" in a kiss or an embrace. You are more likely to recall the physical sensations of your body (e.g., your hands shaking, stomach becoming upset or filled with "butterflies," jaw becoming tight, heart racing), than you are to recall your verbal thoughts.

If you can't recall a situation, try to pay attention the next time you have the experience. Remember, you are observing the thoughts that occur DURING the emotional experience not the thoughts that led up to it, nor the thoughts that occurred after the energies subsided. Paying attention to the thoughts preceding the emotional experience is important for another reason and task, namely, for the purpose of recognizing the triggers leading to emotional states in order to intercept, divert, or even simply to observe the course they take, and their impact on your life. We'll deal with this in more detail later in this chapter.

Emotions are very powerful tools that we are hardwired to use throughout life. They serve as a sort of barometer or thermometer, reading the temperature and/

tion-skills-a-powerful-link

In your feelings...

or pressure of our environment and letting us know how we should engage and/or avoid certain things and situations in life. Similar to how we need to know how to read thermometers and barometers, we have to learn to read and interpret our emotions; how else will we maximize the benefit of having these tools. And just like a barometer or thermometer, we can actually be harmed by neglecting, or incorrectly reading and/or interpreting the information being reported; in this context, the information is emotion.

The perplexing thing about emotions is that they are fluid, meaning, the same experience does not necessarily create the same emotional response in different people; sometimes the emotional response to the same stimuli can vary even within the same person. This often depends on the context in which the stimulation is taking place, the person and/or thing generating the stimulation (including their history and experience with the source), and even how the individual already feels in that moment.

The cognitive and physiological connection behind every emotion is designed, in part, to put your body into auto-pilot as a means to quick action or inaction. This is the reason for the inverse relationship between emotionality and cognitive functioning, meaning, the reason why we don't necessarily "think clearly" during highly emotional states; if a situation truly warrants high emotion, then it is time to take action, not contemplate the situation. For example, imagine you are walking through a dark alley and something moves in the dumpster up ahead. Immediately you feel the sensation of adrenaline being released from your adrenal glands. Your stomach turns, your breathing becomes rapid and shallow, your pupils dilate, your mouth becomes dry, and your ears seem to stick out more (you may even slightly turn your head to point an ear in the direction of the sound).[31] Your body is preparing to take

---

31   All responses of the autonomic nervous system (ANS).

one of three actions: fight, flee, or freeze, as you attempt to neutralize the potential threat.

If a cat jumps out of the dumpster and runs in the opposite direction, the initial fear response might change into a feeling of relief, happiness, or even embarrassment. However, if the noise from the dumpster ends up being a zombie, then the fear is likely to escalate and, based on the individual's training and conditioning (including their life experiences), will result in one of the "3 F's" mentioned before. As you can see, the range of emotional response and reaction is heavily dependent on sensation, perception, learning, consciousness, and personality.

Emotions are motivators. Looking closely, we find the concept of motion actually embedded in the word.[32] In this respect, e-motions are simply psychic energies that move. The direction of this movement is based on how we perceive and interpret, relate and respond to, the source and experience of, the stimulation. If we find the experience pleasant, we may find our selves drawn towards the source; if unpleasant, we may move away in avoidance of the source. If pleasurable but out of context (like a public kiss in the workplace), it may generate feelings of discomfort and awkwardness, leading to a withdrawal similar to when experiencing unpleasant stimuli.

The source of stimulation can be internal and/or external. Internal sources are our own thoughts, imaginings, memories, and even physical sensations related to our bodily processes and functions. Every emotion is usually some combination of all of these things, in various configurations, and often involve external sources as well.

External sources come in the form of sensory-perceptions, meaning, they are something that we hear, see, touch, smell, taste or sense otherwise, and the subsequent perceptions of the same. These external stimuli (noise in

---

32   "moti-" as found in motivation, motion, and motive.

In your feelings...

the dumpster) are then coupled with the internal mechanisms (memories generated by binge watching *The Walking Dead* last night), creating an experience that includes an emotional response (fear), and the accompanying thought (there might be a zombie in the dumpster).

Another example is a person who remembers receiving flowers, chocolates, and gifts from an intimate partner. Recalling the smell of the flowers, the taste of the chocolates, and imagining the sweet words on the card, can all bring back feelings of joy, happiness, security, desire, and pride. The memory is an internal stimuli, based on past external realities, triggering the present emotion.

Similarly, a person can walk down a busy city street and pass by an individual who is wearing the same perfume their mother wears. This external stimulus may trigger memories of their mother and thus generate related emotions based on their experiences with their mother. This is an example of how the external stimulus (smell), interacts with an internal stimulus (memory) to inform the emotion. Based on these interactions, between internal and external stimuli, we are motivated to move in a way consistent with our perception or interpretation of these experiences. This was demonstrated by the cat or zombie in the dumpster example provided above.

It is important to understand how external stimulation via sensory perception, and how it interacts with internal mechanisms (i.e., memory, thoughts, etc.), relates to the context in which the stimuli is experienced. In other words, *where* the stimuli is experienced, along with *when* it is experienced, the *source* of the experience, *how* the experience takes place, and everything else about the situation, influences the response to the situation. Stated more plainly via analogy: A person at a baseball game may enjoy and even expect loud cheering from the crowd. This exact same cheering would likely make them uncomfortable, maybe even fearful, if it were to take place on a subway train. The context matters.

Let's agree that cheering at a ballgame is "normal," and thus, does not naturally cause alarm, unless totally unexpected. However, if someone attending the game has experienced trauma at a previous baseball game, directly associated with the cheering, they may find themselves reacting like the person on a subway train when the cheering begins (this is an example of classical conditioning explained in the chapter on learning). This shows how the context created by the internal mechanisms (experience-based memory, or classical conditioning in this case), has a major influence on perception, interpretation, and ultimately, the emotionally-driven behavior response to the stimulation.

Ancient wisdom teaches that nothing has a value in and of itself, it's all relative; meaning, value is totally dependent on how things and/or conditions interact with other things and/or conditions. In the case of our emotions, we tend to react based on these relationships and interactions, and are typically unaware this is happening. This means we are constantly comparing stimuli to our previously encountered experiences, knowledge and current perceptions of the stimulation, in order to place a value on the experience, and thus respond accordingly. Gaining a solid understanding of this concept will help to decrease susceptibility to having unconscious and unintentional reactions to things, while also helping to avoid the errors of false beliefs and the various forms of dilemma associated with these reactions.

In another example, the internal stimuli (i.e., thought, visualization, "memory") can be totally independent of any real external experience (past or present) and still have an equally powerful impact on the emotional state. Many have experienced worry or concern about

In your feelings...

something that has not happened. Some will ruminate, over and over again, about a particular situation they feel may one day take place, but has never actually happened. These people can sometimes get themselves so emotionally worked up that it actually hinders their ability to function with any level of efficiency and effectiveness. The condition known as obsessive-compulsive disorder (OCD) is an extreme, but well known, example of how this mechanism works.

An individual experiencing OCD, has recurring thoughts (visual and/or verbal) about some potential situation that may or may not be a present reality. These "obsessive" thoughts lead to, and may actually be generated by, feelings of anxiety, worry, concern, and/or fear that this thing they are thinking about is actually real, or will soon become real, and has dire consequences. This then leads to some sort of behavior pattern they feel "compelled" to perform, which will often temporarily relieve some of the anxiousness. It's important to understand that these are coping behaviors, performed as an attempt to relieve the emotions and physical sensations associated with the thoughts. In other words, they are meaningful, purposeful, and oft times found to be beneficial; temporarily alleviating the emotional distress.

For example, a person with OCD may worry about leaving their door unlocked once they have left home for work. In almost ritual fashion, they will drive a certain distance, ruminating over whether to turn around, wondering if they actually left it unlocked, and what might happen if they did leave it unlocked. They'll keep going until the anxiety is so great that they have to return home to check. Some do the same thing based on a fear that they left the stove or iron on, or the dog outside, or the cat inside, etc. The fear is not always irrational, meaning it can be based on some sort of real experience of the past or some very real potential for the present or the future. The trouble is their fixation on the thought, the resulting emotion (anxiety), and the behaviors that follow. It can be counterproductive and damaging to social, professional, and personal well-being.

This last example is perhaps the most difficult to deal with because emotions in this category tend to be based solely on internal stimuli, with only the resulting emotion-based behaviors being tangible and observable. Many of these internal thoughts can be traced to something the individual was exposed to via direct personal experience or indirectly by way of a television show, read in a book, or overheard in a conversation. These vicarious exposures can either be consciously or unconsciously internalized, thereby building up the context within which future thoughts and experiences are measured and interpreted. Regardless of context and degree of experience, the emotions thus triggered, are real enough to impact the person's external and internal reality.

I've often stated "Fear is the most debilitating emotion and anger the most destructive. When you combine the two, devastation is not far behind." Consistent with this saying, Dr. Frances Cress Welsing and Mr. Neely Fuller, Jr. have tirelessly worked to help people to understand the "what" and "why" of racism/White Supremacy,[33] a system thought to be based on emotional distress. According to Dr. Welsing, the unconscious fear, maintained by Whites, of no longer existing as a race, is what drives the system of racism/White supremacy. You can hear affirmations of her perspective echoing through the Charlottesville protests during the Summer of 2017, as marchers exclaimed "We will not be replaced." You can see it in patterns of behavior during the lynchings of the

---

33   Fuller would say he explains the "what" while Dr. Welsing explains the "why." I think each of them did a lot of both.

In your feelings...

late 1800s and early 1900s, when American African male lynching victims were physically castrated, and even in present day behaviors where the reproductive capabilities of non-Whites are being chemically assaulted.[34]

The fallout from these assaults may not be readily understood as such. For example, there was recently a story floating around social media about a small village in the Dominican Republic where "Little Girls Turn Into Boys."[35] Aside from being a misleading title, because little girls are not turning into boys, the article neglected to mention any real viable cause explaining why male children were being born with suppressed sexual features, making them appear to be female. This motivated me to further research why these male children experienced a blockage of testosterone while in the womb, making them incapable of showing recognizable sex traits until they reach puberty (this is when the next surge of testosterone is experienced). Apparently, it is this lack of testosterone and the resulting suppression of penis and testicular formation and growth, led to the male children being raised as females.

The forensic psychologist in me immediately started seeking correlations to such reproductive issues, and almost instantly thought of environmental racism. Of course the article mentioned nothing of the extreme levels of environmental pollutants and toxins, released into the soil and water sources by certain industries mining the island's resources; however, I didn't have to dig too deeply to find it myself. Mention of this would help to appropriately contextualize the developmental occurrence as an

---

34   By lynchmobs and OBGYNs alike (in the form of hysterectomies, chemical castration via legal and illicit drugs, encouraging of abortions and tubal ligations, or even the diminishing of the quality of reproductive cells via toxins unleashed via pollution in certain neighborhoods, known as environmental racism).

35   www.telegraph.co.uk/science/2016/03/12/the-astonishing-village-where-little-girls-turn-into-boys-aged-1/

environmentally induced birth-defect, which is directly related to foreign companies polluting the environment via their mining for gold and other valuable resources. It just so happens that these industries are owned by European and Canadian corporations. The same atrocities exist, although with different outcomes in Sierre Leone with her diamonds, the Congo with her rubber trees and coltan, and Nigeria with her oil.

In almost direct contrast to the global assault on the reproductive capabilities of non-Whites, there are European nations that promote and reward conception and having babies. The successful *"Do It For Denmark!"* campaign[36] is an excellent example. They actually incentivize conception, by offering, amongst other things, three years worth of diapers to couples that successfully conceive while on vacation. Their birth rate in 2013 was 10 per every 1000; Germany's is similar. They expected a baby boom of 1200 babies in the summer of 2016 as a result.[37] What does this have to do with emotions? I am glad you asked. Recall that emotions are directly related to motivation. So much of what takes place on a social and political level, is motivated by emotions;[38] in these examples, as theorized by Dr. Frances Cress Welsing, there tends to be a combination of fear and anger related to concerns of genetic survival by Whites and European nations.

Mr. Fuller says that racism/White supremacy is the number one motivator in the known universe, seconded by sex. If we pay close attention to the rallies, protests, demonstrations, and public displays of discontent, the vast

---

36   https://www.washingtonpost.com/news/morning-mix/wp/2014/03/27/do-it-for-denmark-campaign-wants-danes-to-have-more-sex-a-lot-more-sex/?utm_term=.59b61a59a517
37   www.independent.co.uk/news/world/europe/denmark-s-bizarre-series-of-sex-campaigns-lead-to-baby-boom-a7062466.html
38   Either a reaction to emotion or an attempt to create a reaction to emotions.

majority of them are directly related to racism/White supremacy, although it is only recently that it has received the appropriate labeling. Running a close second are those rallies and demonstrations related to sex: be it gender equality or gender inclusion, reproductive rights, or legalization of same-sex marriage. Even these sex/gender lines tend to be drawn with a colored pencil (meaning there is almost always a race-based element to them).

We'll further explore the relationship between emotions and activism later in this chapter, for now, let's delve a little deeper into how emotions are expressed, the anatomical and physiological mechanisms behind their expression, and how psychology has evolved to manipulate both emotions and their wide range of expression.

As mentioned earlier, the autonomic nervous system (ANS) plays a major role in the external and physiological expression of emotions. Just as the name implies, the ANS is responsible for the actions and functions that take place automatically, meaning, without the need for conscious awareness, direction, and initiation of the processes. Heart rate, breathing, pupil dilation and constriction, patterns of circulation, and involuntary muscle tension, are all examples of processes governed by the ANS.

The two branches of the ANS, the Sympathetic Nervous System (SNS) and the Parasympathetic Nervous System (PNS), are responsible for the physiology related to action and inaction respectively. The SNS usually kicks in when there is a fight or flight situation at hand (the noise in the dumpster). Increased heart rate, dilation of pupils, etc., are all indications of the SNS being activated. The SNS is the branch of the ANS that expends the body's energy reserves. When the SNS kicks in, the body tightens up and may feel jittery. When the excitement is over, the body relaxes and the person may feel "spent." This is the time when the PNS kicks in and restores the body to its

Practical Psychology 101

resting and replenished state. In perpetually "high-stress" situations, the SNS may become overactive, keeping the body tense, making stress the new "norm." This is where stress earns its infamous title: "the silent killer." Keeping the body in an excited state taxes the body and its systems to the point of destruction and impairment.[39]

The following is the best illustration I've heard regarding the excessive state of perpetual stress experienced by humans:

In the animal kingdom, there are stressors everywhere, especially for anything other than the apex predators. For instance, gazelles are thought to experience high levels of stress when being stalked by a lion.

The lion triggers the "flight" response, where the gazelle's sympathetic nervous system (SNS), on a scale of zero-to-ten, is on ten! It is literally running for its life. Once it has successfully evaded the pursuing lion, and the "fear" subsides, the gazelle returns to its resting state, and the parasympathetic nervous system (PNS) returns the body to a state of homeostasis–peaceful equilibrium.

The difference with humans is we will continue to think and talk about how that lion almost ate us for the next 10 years. We will celebrate stress by constantly reliving the moments, posting about it on social media, posting selfies with the pursuing lion in the background, or "going live" right then and there. This can keep our bodies perpetually in fight, flight, or freeze mode, with the SNS in full swing; never allowing the PNS a chance to return us to a healthy baseline. This also applies to the constant viewing of traumatic videos or listening to violent music.

Perceiving an environment as dangerous, especially when it is our home, our neighborhood, or place of employment, contributes to the excessive experiencing of stress, and the subsequent deterioration of our physical

---

39   http://www.apa.org/helpcenter/stress-body.aspx

In your feelings...

and mental health. This is related to Post Traumatic Stress Disorder (PTSD), which is called "Post Traumatic Slave Syndrome" (PTSS)[40], when specific to the enslavement of Africans and victims of racism/White supremacy. PTSS highlights the impact of trans-generational trauma, which Western science has recently "discovered" may be passed along from parent to child via the sperm.[41]

Dick Gregory, in an interview on *Democracy Now* (February, 2002), stated the following about fear:

> You know, fear is a gift from God. Fear is supposed to last a few minutes. Fear will make you hear something and you'll run through a plate glass window and will not get cut. Fear is what make a mother walk out in the garage and see that this car had fallen off those stilts and fell on the baby, and she'll pick that car up. But that fear is supposed to last a few minutes. And when that fear lasts longer than a few minutes, then it destroys you internally because you are on automatic pilot...
>
> You know there is a legend that says thousands of years ago "The Plague" was supposed to go into Afghanistan, no I'm sorry Baghdad, that's the way the story goes, and kill 5,000 people. "The Plague" went in and 50,000 people died. So they was questioning "The Plague," and they said, "I thought you was going into Baghdad and kill 5,000 people, what happened?" He said, "I did. I just killed 5,000. The rest died from fright."

In each of my spiritual initiations, there has been a clear statement and objective to master one's emotions. Mastery of emotions is what sets you apart from the emotionally-driven masses. Don't get me wrong, emotions are not a bad thing. I have demonstrated their use, role, and many purposes in the earlier parts of this chapter; they

---

40   Drs. Joy Degruy and Patricia Newton are two scholars who have advanced our understanding of these concepts.
41   https://www.the-scientist.com/?articles.view/articleNo/39695/title/Traces-of-Trauma-in-Sperm-RNA/

can, however, become a liability if a person is excessively driven by emotions, and constantly succumbs to their influence and dominance, especially at the expense of their many other ways of knowing and functioning. Again, they are excellent tools to be used while navigating life, and should always be respected, and "at the ready" to intervene in those moments where their form and function is the optimal means for resolution, but otherwise kept in check.

The interpretation and mastery of emotional expression is where practical psychology comes into play. Being able to correctly read a person's emotions via their body language, facial expression, stance, posture, gait, hand positioning, and eye movement, can mean the difference between life and death. Being able to read a situation accurately, being able to discern the energy radiating from an individual, a collective of people, or an event, and distinguishing it from your own, provides clarity of mind, which in turn, promotes good judgment and decision making.

I have often wondered if any of the nine victims murdered at Emanuel African Methodist Episcopal Church,[42] in South Carolina, felt an emotional indication of what was about to take place as Dylan Roof entered their sacred space. I wonder if anyone could feel the murderous intentions that must have been emanating from him, as he took a seat patiently waiting to unleash his wrath on the unsuspecting worshipers.

In situations like this, if someone did feel a threat, they may have dismissed it out of a lack of confidence in acknowledging, respecting, and acting on these feelings in a conscious and intentional way. Another related reason, why someone who has sensed a threat may not act on it, is out of fear of offending the person they are reacting to,

42   Interesting that "Mother Emanuel" was founded by Morris Brown, and was the place of spiritual refuge for Denmark Vesey as he planned a revolt against racism/White supremacy, set for June 22, 1822 (literally 195 years, to the day, before Roof's attack).

In your feelings...

just in case their feelings are wrong. This is why it is of extreme importance to learn how to interpret emotions and to eventually master them. Get to the point that you'd rather be wrong following your insight, than wrong for denying or ignoring it. This could literally save your life.

In the legal and forensic world, observing, paying attention to, and proper interpretation of subtle cues, separates good interrogators from bad ones; the good ones, because of this skill, are more capable of understanding the mental state of their subject, based on their knowledge of emotions, body language, and facial expressions.

Whether a quick twitch of the corner of the mouth, or a slight raising of the eyebrows, our faces can indicate our emotional state, beyond our conscious control. We use this tool daily, consciously or unconsciously. For example, children watch and study their parents' body language in order to know their mood. In social settings, like a party or club scene, people subtly read the body language of others when deciding whether to approach someone or to leave them alone. Folks get and give mixed signals all the time, while others clearly ignore the obvious in their pursuits; perhaps they should take a course in practical psychology and improve their awareness.

On the manipulation side of things, the "pick up artists" of the world learn how to not only read body language, but to also use body language to influence and sometimes control the emotions of those they are seducing and targeting. Therapists are taught the same thing, however, instead of targeting and seducing, therapists mirror their clients and patients in order to increase their level of comfort while in session; different means, different goals (hopefully), but the same science.

In the court room, good attorneys also know how to use emotions in order to get an opposing person to say things they otherwise would rather keep unspoken, or even push them until they have an emotional breakdown while on the stand; this tactic is sometimes used to paint a certain picture of their credibility as a witness, or to prove their emotional state is volatile and therefore, capable of the accusations. Referring back to the episode of *Power* where the attorney Terry Silver, played by Brandon Victor Dixon, warned James St. Patrick against appearing to be an "angry Black man" on the stand. Remember, he later had a real example to point out when a police detective, a Black male, broke under the pressure of an emotionally-charged cross examination. It's all connected.

This is an important area where we can benefit from learning practical psychology, especially those who are involved in social justice movements. If the American African detective mentioned above was trained to control his emotions, he would have been less susceptible to the tactics of the defense attorney, who in the moment, was trying to prove that the detective was actually a more viable suspect for the murder charges than his client.

Mastery of emotions is what places "choice" between experiences and your response to them. Emotional control is what allows us to avoid unnecessary and sometimes damaging "knee-jerk" reactions to situations, by granting us the opportunity to employ our *higher-order thinking*, also known as *executive cognitive functioning*, to regulate potentially emotionally-charged thoughts, speech, and actions.

Think about this as it relates to the many videos circulating of American Africans being discriminated against, facing race-based harassment, or otherwise unjustly treated. In many of these videos, the victim is often displaying high levels of emotion that is easily recognized in their tone of voice, the statements being made, and even by their physical appearance (crying, looking visibly shaken and/or hurt). This is never the optimal way to

In your feelings...

handle such situations because it can lead to unnecessary and avoidable physical conflict (being brutalized by police officers) and/or impeding one's ability to clearly articulate their case, and perhaps, keeping the victim from simply leaving the hostile situation because of the "need" to emote and be heard in the moment.

It would have been perfect if the students at Howard University demonstrated emotional control in their encounter with what I perceive to be race-baiting behaviors of the White female high schoolers, when they entered the student center wearing "Make America Great Again" hats.[43] One Howard student allegedly took the hat off one of the girls' head. Others verbally confronted them. Even if none of this was hostile, there is still a strategic way to handle these types of encounters that will serve to protect the individual and the institution.

My immediate insights and thoughts led me to believe this was a concerted effort to set-up and race-bait American Africans into appearing to be racist and hostile, when in actuality they are the victims of the same. As I predicted, the story being told is that the Howard students were racist and aggressive towards these innocent high school girls who were simply looking for a place to eat while visiting Washington, D.C.[44]

In my training with The Ausar Auset Society, I learned of the ancient Egyptian (Kemetic) concept of Men Ab, literally meaning a "stable heart." This concept and practice is used to do what I have described above: grant mastery of response to any potentially, emotionally charged situation. This does not mean that a person functions in an emotionless manner. On the contrary, a person

---

43   www.essence.com/news/two-white-women-howard-university-make-america-great-again

44   www.aol.com/article/news/2017/08/22/white-teenage-girls-claim-they-were-harassed-at-howard-university-for-wearing-make-america-great-again-hats-hbcu/23157174/

will function with a higher sensitivity to emotions, both their own and those of another. This heightened sensitivity serves to make the individual more empathic, more situationally aware, and more able to produce the appropriate and chosen response to any given situation. They will become more aware when a particular emotion is coming on. This gives them the ability to foreshadow and predict responses and reactions, as well as granting a sense of self-awareness that will give an advance notice of how they are about to feel.

African psychology deals with emotions in the form of the various personalities mentioned in the next chapter related to the "Tree of Life," the Neteru, or the Orisha. Each of these principles come with a disposition to express certain emotions more than others, and this is based on a specific configuration of temperature and humidity, which yields one of the four elements (Air, Earth, Fire, Water). An example of this, as you will soon see, is how the fiery types are more likely to display emotions on the scale of courage, ranging from cowardice to bold. The practice of Men Ab is what gives intentional and clear access to the emotions and personalities that are not your "natural" disposition, or currently conditioned response.

The motivation aspect of emotion is directly linked to our discussion on learning, specifically to reinforcements. These reinforcers are categorized as *needs*, *drives*, and *incentives*, and are collectively called *motives*. As mentioned, Freud claims sex as the number one motivator; Mr. Neely Fuller, Jr. places sex second to racism/White supremacy. For the sake of clarity, we will spend a little time describing needs, drives, and incentives, and how they operate to motivate.

A *need* is typically based on a real or perceived lack, with physiological needs being based on some form of deprivation: hunger is a result of being food/nourishment

In your feelings...

deprived; sleep is a need that stems from depletion of energy reserves, thereby being deprived of energy; the need to inhale arises from the deprivation of fresh oxygen in the lungs/blood. There are also needs that do not necessarily link directly to a state of deprivation, but are always linked to the well-being and survival of the organism. These include the need to eliminate waste, the need to avoid pain, the need for a comfortable environment, etc.

You may have noticed that all of these are related to a physiological state. There are also needs that are purely psychological in nature, including: the need for power, belonging, social contact, success, the need to be needed, wanted, desired, the need to be right, the need to be seen, the need to be acknowledged, and so forth.

These too, are connected with a sense of deprivation, or lack. Mr. Neely Fuller, Jr. talks about these in terms of the need to compensate, leading to what he calls "compensatory behavior." Understanding needs is important because both psychological and physiological needs can be used to manipulate and control thoughts, speech, and/or actions. This use is directly related to the fear of not being able to fulfill one's needs, or the deep sense of deprivation which leads to a higher susceptibility to being manipulated and coerced based on these needs.

We see community leaders manipulated based on their needs all the time. The community leader that is driven by a need to be seen, can be manipulated by offers to appear in certain public forums; they can be manipulated by empty offers that appease their Ego. In relationships, the person that has a need to be desired can also be manipulated into doing and/or accepting certain behaviors if their partner deems it to be more desirable; the fulfillment of, or meeting the needs of another, often comes with a degree of emotional satisfaction, which serves as its own reward.

Practical Psychology 101

Think about the happy dance some people do when they are eating their favorite food; or how a dog's tail wags with excitement at the site and sound of their food being placed into the bowl. This is the result of specific pleasure-related neurotransmitters being released, and certain brain centers being stimulated in response to the fulfillment of certain needs.

The natural consequence to having needs is the presence of *drives*. In short, a drive is the movement towards fulfilling a need. It's what a need activates. Just like with needs, there are both psychologically and physiologically-based drives, both designed to fulfill their related needs. To ignite the drives is the purpose of intentionally depriving an organism and thereby, creating needs.

When training a dog, as mentioned in the learning chapter, it is easier to get them to perform a specific behavior for a treat if they are hungry; the treat fulfills the need for food and nourishment, this need is what drives the behavior of obedience to command. It is important to understand this concept to the point of being able to translate these examples into situations related to social justice movements and other forms of activism.

Many social justice movements are developed based on a need for justice, which itself is based on the perception that a particular group has been grossly deprived of their rights (justice), either by being mistreated, or overlooked. These needs develop into an energy that eventually moves (e-motion: e = energy, motion = movement) people into action; activism. Needs and drives can be intentionally created, and the means to fulfill these needs also created, to serve the needs of the one responsible for the deprived state in the first place.

Again, refer to the hungry dog that is purposely kept from eating, in order that they may be more readily and easily trained. Time and time again, we see examples

In your feelings...

of how a "leader" generates loyalty by giving their "followers" just enough to maintain loyalty, but not enough to ever be fully satisfied. I recently saw an example of this in the movie *A Bronx Tale*.

There is a scene where *Sonny* (played by Chazz Palminteri) is schooling *Calogero* or *C* (played by Lillo Brancato) about how it is better to be "feared" than "loved." He talks about how he stays in the neighborhood so the community feels protected by his presence. This sense of protection comes from examples of *Sonny's* potential to become physically violent towards those he deems to be a threat against what he cares about. The fear that keeps others motivated to remain loyal to him comes from their need to avoid pain, and the proximity of the possibility of experiencing pain, of which *Sonny's* presence is a constant reminder. Dictators erect statues of themselves amongst their oppressed populations for this very reason.

The third aspect of motivation is *incentive*. Incentives are neither needs, nor drives, but carry traits of both. An incentive is often desirable on its own accord, however, they may also fulfill a need. An incentive is usually related to some sort of comfort, some form of pleasure, and/or some type of reduction in drive. An incentive can be an object, a person, and/or a situation, all of which are deemed desirable to the person being offered, even if the desirability is linked to the removal of something unpleasant and unwanted (recall negative reinforcement from the chapter on learning). Just about anything can be "incentivized." Incentives can appeal to the Id, Ego, and/or the Super Ego of a person, in that they can entice the base desires of the personality, and/or things related to the individual's sense of self, and morality.

The inherent power of incentives, needs, and drives can all be harnessed by anyone skilled enough to recognize them on a subtle level. People can be incentivized into loy-

Practical Psychology 101

alty by the promise of a promotion, better than standard treatment, financial raises and/or bonuses, etc. A person can be manipulated into betrayal by these very same things. People can be convinced to totally neglect their own personal pursuits and desires, and to give it all to a social movement based on their needs and drives, especially when properly incentivized. Religious movements tend to carry the strongest incentive of all—the gifts associated with pleasing God.[45] The believer who is told that certain behaviors and attitudes will more swiftly and assuredly place them into the grace of God, is capable of anything. Think about suicide bombers that literally give their lives in the name of God, and those who give up all of their wealth and "free will" to their religious organization.

A leader that knows the needs and drives of their followers, and who is also skilled in offering appropriate incentives, is more likely to gain and maintain loyalty, while simultaneously decreasing the likelihood of disloyalty and betrayal. This is key to maintaining momentum and longevity in social justice movements. It is a delicate balance because satisfying a need can eliminate the drive and bring about stagnation, therefore, a certain degree of "hunger" is necessary to keep people moving. Many take this philosophy on as their personal means of staying self-motivated and driven.

Emotion and motivation are literally at the core of why people do what they do. This is the reason why the court Jester is thought to be the most powerful person in the King's court; yes, even more powerful than the King and Queen. The Jester is the one skilled in emotional manipulation; they are the master's of that craft. In a thoughtful Kingdom, the royal family is trained in the

---

45   These types of incentives typically appeal to the Super Ego by fulfilling an individual's need for morality and approval from a higher power, i.e., God.

In your feelings...

ability to control their emotions as described earlier in this chapter, and thus, are impervious to the manipulations of the Jester. They stand beyond the grasp of unconscious emotional persuasion and manipulation. They are the ones who are skilled in the use of incentives, needs, and drives to control and otherwise guide others: their subjects.

The best leaders, good or bad, are those who have developed the skill and ability to persuade people to follow with minimal resistance, and a minimum amount of thought involved as they execute orders. Whether Adolf Hitler or Dr. Martin Luther King, Jr., Malcolm X or David Duke, effective leadership and social activism is always measured, at least in part, by the ease with which people are motivated to follow.

Protecting your emotional state, and minimizing your susceptibility to being manipulated by the emotional states and desires of others should be a priority for anyone seeking to participate in social justice movements. Maintaining emotional awareness, executive cognitive function, and the tools necessary for emotional regulation puts the social activist beyond the perils of certain knee-jerk reactions, especially those strategically imposed by planned disruptions. Distinguishing between your feelings and those of another will help you to process and let go of the negative baggage that easily accumulates and becomes the normalized stress that many, who are facing injustice, too readily internalize, and claim as their own.

As a true champion for social justice, one should seek to guard their emotions, master them, and then totally control what motivates your behaviors. To be impenetrable to the incentives offered by others will render you less manipulable, and therefore, keep you from being a liability to the movement and your organization, when others seek to entice you from your mission and purpose.

A very effective and practical method for maintaining emotional control is to first be able to recognize the emotions prior to them manifesting fully in your person. This is done by paying attention to how your emotions progress from an initial thought, belief, or action, into the eventual emotion taking root in your being. Some of us will be triggered by an experience that then creates a thought, which then makes us feel some way. Sometimes it is a thought, that leads to an experience, which is then followed by an emotion. Regardless of the order, it is important for us to first increase our awareness, then seek to disrupt the circuit as soon as possible. This is done by resisting the thought, reinterpreting the thought, and/ or by going in a completely opposite direction from where the thought is trying to send you.

Another major aspect is to control your breathing when in the midst of an emotional experience. Our breathing shifts according to the emotion we are experiencing. Maintaining a deep, slow, and rhythmic breathing pattern makes it more difficult for the emotion to exist, and definitely less likely to take control. This is one of the major keys to meditation, yoga, and other ancient healing arts.

Emotional mastery is a skill acquired in the early stages of any true system of initiation and self-improvement. This is a protective measure, designed to safeguard us from carelessly handling the powers that come with acquiring self-knowledge. For those of us interested in social activism, we would only increase our benefit to ourselves, our causes, and those who we are working with and for, by increasing our emotional competency. We will become more powerful by our ability to control the direction of our emotions and our effortless channeling of those energies towards more beneficial and positive outcomes. To be able to emote, at will, makes one a very powerful force to be reckoned with; it is the hallmark of self-discipline, and the key to greatness.

Chapter 7
Know thyself...

T ypically when two people meet, and are trying to "get to know" each other, they usually ask for a name, perhaps an occupation, and maybe even information about where they're from.[46] Aside from this, there may be some small talk, but rarely is there any deeper exploration into who the person really is, or a conscious and intentional evaluation of their personality traits and characteristics.

Fortunately, socializers of today don't have to worry much about the initial meeting and the grunge work of getting to know someone; the world-wide-web has you covered. Between social media sites, a quick Google search, and on-line dating, the internet pretty much provides all of this information and more. We are so accessible these days that you can even track daily movements of a complete stranger who just so happens to be part of the same social network as you. Stalker much? All of this fascinating technology is based in psychology. Yup. There are dating sites that actually boast of great success due to their ability to generate psychological profiles and increase "matching" accuracy using complex personality assessments.

To the trained eye, having access to a person's social media posts and profile, presents a gold mine of data

---

46   Mr. Neely Fuller, Jr. suggests no less than 100 questions when you first meet someone, and definitely before becoming intimate with them. He recommends this approach in order to minimize the confusion and unpleasant surprises that almost always show up later.

and information, exposing their personality, habits, tendencies, and even things tucked away in their unconscious mind. Fortunately, or unfortunately, many are not trained in this important skill. I say fortunately because with this skill, one can easily manipulate others; I say unfortunately because without it, people can draw false conclusions and/ or miss some very valuable information that is hidden in plain sight.

For some cultures, responding to the question, "Who are you?" can be a complex experience. The answer can go well beyond superficial characteristics, and may include the names of several Ancestors, their tribal, neighborhood, and/or hometown affiliation, a mention of their life purpose and several other key pieces of information. All of this is important and contributes to the totality of who they are. In the 1970s, and even in some current subcultures, the respondent may have also included their zodiac sign in order to acknowledge the heavenly influence of the stars on their personality.[47]

We are currently deep into the "Information Age," and can choose to be knowledgeable and informed about a great number of things. It is my opinion that every person would greatly benefit from a sincere exploration of self. Yes, it is important to be learned in many worldly things, however, self-knowledge trumps it all. When going through grad school, I made a deal with myself to read five pages of text related to "self-knowledge" for every one page I read related to my academic pursuits. I also chose to spend the majority of my time outside of academia studying and seeking more knowledge, insight, practical experience, and wisdom, related to "self-knowledge."

My initial intention was to maintain a healthy balance between the Eurocentric curriculum associated

---

47   Think of the R & B song "Float On" and that Earth, Wind, and Fire album cover with the zodiac symbols.

with my advance degrees and my overall African sense
of self. As an unintended by-product, I also developed
a sense of empowerment, and gained access to spiritual
power and cultural tools that would serve me later in life.
In hindsight, I now realize that this so-called "by-product"
is actually the ultimate goal for many self-development
quests. It's too bad there aren't more people, worldwide,
with these tools and a deep knowledge of who they are.
The lack of spiritually evolved people is because many
have not been challenged to seek a deeper understanding,
nor have they been informed of the power that rests in the
knowledge of knowing who you are, at the deepest levels
of identity.

Family lineage and genetic inheritance plays a
major role in identity and personality development.[48] It
provides both the natural disposition as well as the context
within which socialization will take place (nature and nurture, respectively). The external expression of one's genes
(i.e., phenotype) is what sets up environmental responses
from, and thus a person's interactions with, society. In other words, how you look can and often does influence the
way society, as a whole, will interact and respond to you.
Just think about racial, sexual, and/or gender discrimination to get a clear illustration of this point.

We all know certain families with "strong genes."
These are the families whose kinfolk are known by the
certain curvature and/or whisk of their eyebrows, their
height, lip or nose shape, large forehead, or small ears;
they are often met with statements like, "I knew you was
one of them Jones kids...I could tell by your eyes."

Hair color & texture, frame and build of one's
natural body, along with stature and even sometimes how
an individual walks and talks, is a function of their family

---

48   The movie *Assassin's Creed* puts an interesting spin on this
concept.

lineage and genetic dispositions. These characteristics and traits are used to judge if someone is pretty, handsome, attractive, repulsive, ignored, adored, engaged, abandoned, ridiculed, supported, denied, embraced, rejected, accepted, made to feel loved or hated, and in far too many cases, whether they are given a warning at a traffic stop, or if they are assaulted and/or lose their life.

Humans tend to be simultaneously superficial and deep. In modern times, it seems that many are conditioned to lean more towards the superficial aspects of their nature, judging based on minimal or partial information, and not taking the time to confirm whether the info is true or totally false. This is often the case when we consider the racially-tense climate that has plagued this nation and the world as a whole. The rhetoric stating that "race" is a myth, is a total farce. It's similar to the rhetoric that states that "Black on Black violence is a myth." Both of these are as real as the words you are reading on this page.

The part that *is* mythical, with both race and intra-racial violence, is the notion that the socio-political distinctions made are somehow a natural occurrence *because of* someone's race. Again, race *is* real, and so is Black-on-Black violence. The myth is found in how intra-racial violence and race are utilized within the socio-political context (i.e., violence is somehow natural and unique to Blacks, and race makes one group naturally inferior [non-Whites] and another naturally superior [Whites]).

Even if they were both absolute myths, meaning, absolutely not real, the concepts could still be weaponized and used to fit an agenda. Any good mental health professional could tell you that both "real" and "perceived" threats are equally threatening, and can both lead to dire and dangerous outcomes. So whether a myth or not, the implications of race and Black-on-Black violence are real.

Racism targets the African phenotype by making

Know thy self...

it seem to be something negative and deplorable. The ease with which this is accomplished, shows just how easily humans can be trained towards the superficial, in spite of having evidence to the contrary. Not only is there evidence showing that the African phenotype is beautiful, adaptive, and having many positive attributes, there is also evidence showing how desired and desirable these features are, especially to those who do not have them naturally. It just so happens that this group also promotes self-hate amongst Africans.

A clear example of this is found in the large amounts of skin-bleaching creams and hair straightening products sold in many predominately African nations (including continental Africa, the Caribbean, Black communities in the U.S., and Central & South America). These chemicals are often used by those who have been taught and/or impacted by the negative treatment they have received, directly or indirectly, for carrying an African phenotype; be it skin color, nose structure, lip thickness, hair texture, body-type, etc. The large amounts of chemical hair treatments and the multi-billion dollar "hair-care" industry also testifies to the truth of this discussion.

Ironically, some Whites will spend large amounts of money: tanning to darken their skin; having plastic surgery or receiving injections to increase the fullness of their lips, buttocks, hips, or otherwise altering their physical features to match what is naturally expressed by the African phenotype; all of this goes on while some Africans risk their lives trying to get rid of the same. Some will go as far as actually pretending to be Black...ask Rachel. This entire phenomenon, when taken as a whole, points to the ego defense mechanism known as *reaction formation.*

Remember, ego defense mechanisms are used to protect the Ego from a difficult reality through diversion, deflection, or otherwise "removing" conscious awareness of the reality. In this case, reaction formation is employed when there is something desired, yet unobtainable. In order to deal with a desire for something they can't have, a person's unconscious mind will pretend that the desired object, thing, or situation is actually repulsive and totally undesirable. Where I'm from, we call this "hating." Dr. Welsing explains much of racist symbolism and behavior to be fueled by this unconscious process. She points out the following cliché's and occurrences as demonstrations verifying the desirability, and sometimes unconsciously perceived superiority, of non-White people by the "dominant," White culture:

> a woman's ideal lover is "tall, **dark**, and handsome;" when a man is expecting a baby (a sign of virility), they are given cigars (big brown phallic symbols), as opposed to cigarettes (small white phallic symbols whose synonym is "fag"); the same is true when a "successful" man is shown smoking, it is usually a cigar or pipe, but rarely a cigarette; the "sexy" color for lingerie and panties is black; most popular candy shared and consumed on Valentine's Day is chocolate; there are two basic categories of ball games: big colored (basketball, football, soccer), and little white (ping pong, golf, cue ball in pool which is used to knock all the colored balls into the green earth).

The desire to have color and to produce color is real; so is the futility of that desire unless there is a person of color participating. This points to the amount of rape that took place during enslavement and post-emancipation, of African women and men, by White women and men; many of which ended in the conception and birth of non-White babies. The popular story was that African men were wanting to rape White women, and that African women were seductresses, on the prowl, manipulating White men into sex.[49] These things may have occurred,

---

49   Birth of a Nation and the way the story of Sally Hemmings is

Know thy self...

and if they did, it was more an exception than it was the rule, especially considering the conditions of slavery.

Just as real as this desire to have and produce color, is the projection of disgust onto those who have naturally occurring skin color and other aspects of the African phenotype. This is verifiable by the mistreatment and negative judgment of those who are darker-skinned, and who have features furthest from the phenotype of Whites. As an example, president Abraham Lincoln was often ridiculed for having "darker skin" by his political opponents. Dr. Bobby Wright discussed this aggression that Whites have towards blackness as the "psychopathic racial personality."

Comprehending the above dialogue regarding race and racism is important because so much of what we take on as our identity, is based upon how the external environment reacts to our presence and how we, in turn, respond or react to that experience. In this regard, there are several social scientists who have developed stage theories of racial identity development, for people of various races, in an attempt to better understand the depth of this phenomenon, and the predictable course it can take.

One such scientist is Dr. W. E. Cross. He developed a stage theory of "Negro to Black" racial identity development called *Nigrescence*. This stage theory details how an individual of African descent goes from "not seeing color," or from not acknowledging race as a factor in their daily lives (Pre-Encounter phase), to having an overt and undeniable experience with racism (Encounter phase), which subsequently sends them on a journey to reconcile their former concept of self, as it relates to race or "racelessness," eventually leading them to understand that they are likely living in an environment steeped in racism/White supremacy.

By the end of this journey, the individual is thought

---

told as some mutual-love-relationship supports this notion.

to emerge with a balanced and healthy perspective of their own racial group, and how it relates to others. Part of this balance is found by accepting both the good and the bad of one's own race, while doing the same for other racial groups.

The need for this reconciliation is due, in part, to White supremacists working diligently, on a global scale, to create a narrative of Africans and their descendants that is full of shame and without glory. This occurs as they simultaneously inflict physical, psychological, and emotional harm, on Africans, while holding their own White racial group as superior and blameless for their actions. By framing the historical relevance of American Africans within the context of enslavement and the struggles that followed, a situation has been created that subtly promotes the rejection of anything to do with African ancestry, and the acceptance of those things that relate more with the "dominant," White, ruling class. Dr. Frances Cress Welsing wrote of this in detail, specifically regarding the color and symbolism of Jesus.[50]

The superficial expressions of identity thus far highlighted are clear indications of a deeper turmoil taking place in the human psyche, similar to how underwater earthquakes are perceptible to those on the surface via wave activity. The changing of physical features, to the point of having surgery or otherwise chemically creating these changes, typically occurs for two basic reasons: 1) dissatisfaction with what they have; or 2) to enhance or change what they have to something they desire more. Amos Wilson points out the necessity of creating and tailoring the desires and "tastes" of the masses, as a means to maintain domination and control.[51]

---

50   See *The Isis Papers: The Keys to the Colors*, chapters 5 and 13
51   See *The Falsification of African Consciousness: Eurocentric History, Psychiatry and the Politics of White Supremacy* by Amos Wilson

Know thy self...

A combination of the aforementioned reasons, is the most likely culprit fueling the mass exodus from "Blackness" found globally amongst non-White people. With so much negative propaganda, disseminated with ever increasing levels of efficiency, effectiveness and sophistication, it makes perfect sense that a large number of non-Whites would seek to alter themselves in order to better identify with Whites. Images of "beauty" are biased towards White features; criminal justice is biased towards White features; employment is biased towards White features; distribution of wealth and resources is biased towards White features. The best thing about this situation is that each of these biases are man-made, therefore, not a natural occurrence. This means an appeal to nature would easily crumble this straw-house of a system. In other words, being proud of who and what you are, after finding out the truth regarding who and what you are, will empower you to operate beyond the pervasive influence of this fragile power structure.

Recall our discussion from the chapter on learning, about how humans avoid punishment and seek pleasure. African people have been punished for being African, while simultaneously, Whites seem to be reaping every known reward and privilege available, simply for being White. It does not take a conscious contemplation of this situation for an individual to equate one to punishment and the other to reward; it will occur unconsciously on its own volition. Once this correlation has been drawn, behaviors begin to slant in the direction of pleasure and reward, i.e., whiteness.

The highly ironic and paradoxical alternative to this phenomenon, *Black Flight*, is the number of Whites rushing to immigrate into "Blackness." This is readily exemplified by those Whites who actually seek to darken or add color to their skin via tattoos, sun bathing, salon-tanning, and even spray on tans. They also do other things to gain what has stereotypically been used for the caricaturization of Africans and their descendants, i.e., Botox treatments for fuller lips, butt implants and squats, braiding, corn-rolling, and dread-locking their hair.

There is a video[52] of a White girl who must be about 6 years old. She is being interviewed by an off-camera, adult female (the assumption is that she is also White and perhaps the girl's mother). The little girl claims with confidence that when she grows up, she wants to be a "Black female, police officer, rapper." The woman tells her she cannot be that because God made her a White girl. By the end of the video, the girl has held her position that she will be a Black woman rapper when she grows up.

I have seen another video of yet another young White girl dealing with her racial identity in a similar manner. This time, the girl exclaimed, very confidently, that she *is* a "Strong Black Woman."[53] I wonder what Dr. Kenneth Clark would have to say about this turn of events. In the words of Sandra Izsadore on her duet with Fela Kuti, *Upside Down*: "Everything upside down."

The remedies to these psychological ailments will likely come from the deeper exploration of personality, identity, and how one chooses to express themselves regardless of societal influences. Modern psychology is full of theories and explanations of how personality and identity are developed. And even has an entire category in psychopathology known as "personality disorders."[54] We will spend the remainder of this chapter exploring some of these theories from various perspectives.

To begin, let us first define personality according

52   https://youtu.be/NQhzGg1-FIA
53   https://youtu.be/zj1imGiuBTU
54   This shows that not all personality is healthy, and that one can function with personality issues as demonstrated by Drs. Bobby Wright, Kobi Kambon, and Na'im Akbar amongst others.

Know thy self...

to Western psychology, after which, we will explore the psychoanalytical perspective (this is the orientation presented in the chapter on consciousness, dealing heavily with the unconscious mind), and finally, we will view personality from the trait perspective. Each perspective will be interwoven with comparisons to, and elaborations via the African-centered lens.

Typically, personality is defined as *a relatively stable pattern of emotions, motives, thinking, and behaviors that can be used to distinguish one person from another*; in other words, those internal psychological processes that make every individual unique. Again, this is the Western psychological perspective and definition of personality. African-centered perspectives, meaning those that ascribe to the African worldview, see personality as a fluid set of psychological and spiritual tools, all of which can be developed and utilized in day-to-day living, simultaneously and individually.

This means that the African-centered perspective acknowledges an innate personality, consisting of a set of dispositions that one develops "naturally" from birth, and according to some traditions, as carryovers from previous lives, as well as from Ancestors of their genetic kin. The African-centered perspective has another very important distinction, namely, it also assumes that the other personality "types" can and should be intentionally developed and utilized. The various "personalities" or tools, are often personified as spiritual beings in the various African wisdom traditions (Orisha, Neteru, Lwa, Angels, Ancestors, Abosum, etc.), and are used as guides for society. We will revisit this concept in more detail later in this chapter.

The psychoanalytic approach is not too far off from the more Ancient African perspective. This should come as no surprise because both Sigmund Freud and his student Carl Gustav Jung spent time studying and seeking to comprehend the various non-Western perspectives of psychology, in the truest sense of the word. This included the study of Nile Valley symbolism, worldview, and spiritual science.[55] Freud took his studies of African spirituality so serious that he adorned his office with statues and images of African Gods (see photo below).

© Freud Museum London

One point of difference between the Western and African perspectives is that the psychoanalytic approach explores personality as the expression of a "battle" between these subtle psychic structures, whereas the African perspective views them as harmonious complements.

Freud called these psychic structures the *Id, Ego* and *Super Ego*. The theory holds the Id as the oldest part of the human personality. It is present from birth, and the basis for human drives (survive, reproduce, etc.), with no concern for how successfully achieving these goals impacts others. The motivations originating in the Id are thought to be totally within the unconscious aspects of awareness. The Id is considered to be volatile, impulsive, and sporadic because it functions based on, and responds to, any and all impulses related to survival, reproduction, and the attraction to pleasure/avoidance of pain principles.

The Id is known to carry major influence over the personality of the individual. In many cases it directly informs the decisions and actions taken by the person in

---

55   See, Jung in Africa (2005) by Blake W. Burleson.

Know thy self...

which it is dominant; stated another way: during those moments when the Id is dominant, observable behaviors will reflect an attempt to satisfy those drives and meeting the needs governed by the Id. This influence is carried out based on the strength of the drive created by the Id's "desire" or "need" to satisfy these goals. Hunger in a pet is an excellent example. It is far easier to train a hungry dog, than it is to train a satiated one. This is because (as mentioned in our discussion on conditioning, reinforcement, and primary needs) hunger is a primary need, and thus, a powerful tool to use for behavior change and modification. Again, the promise of a treat is more motivating to the dog who has not eaten breakfast, than it is to the dog who has just finished a meal. Human behavior is influenced similarly. Desire can be created for a particular product, then access to that product is controlled. Much of marketing is geared towards agitating the Id, which controls and motivates behaviors, beliefs and attitudes, while they seem to be directed by the conscious mind or Ego.[56]

The Id, being totally unconscious, typically functions without the person's awareness of "why" they did what they did, do what they do, desire what they want to do, and/or, in some cases, the fact that they even did or continue to do it. In regards to how the Id reacts or responds to its drive to fulfill basic needs, we find it to be fairly easy to program. Instrumental to this programming is the insertion of definitions and conceptualizations of what is considered threatening, pleasurable, painful, punishing, and rewarding. We covered this in the learning chapter. As we now know, two people can view the exact same situation in two very different ways. One might see storm clouds gathering as a romantic situation. Another, may see it as the scariest thing ever.

These perspectives are developed overtime, and

---

56   See Tom Burrell's *Brainwashed*.

are based on the natural disposition of the person, their direct or indirect experience with similar situations, and what they believe about the current version of the situation. If the second person in the above example is from New Orleans and has survived the aftermath of Hurricane Katrina, or from Houston and survived Hurricane Harvey, or even from St. Kitts & Nevis, or Dominica, and survived the wrath of Hurricane Irma, they will likely see the clouds gathering and think of how these storms began. They may be hyper-vigilant, meaning, they may be responding to the trauma of Harvey, Irma or Katrina, as opposed to the situation at hand; preparing for a hurricane when in actuality, there is only a summer shower brewing on the horizon.

The first person's perspective may be based on childhood memories of dancing in the rain with his siblings, or seeing her parents hugging and kissing in a very nurturing way while sitting on the porch during a storm. This example demonstrates how our reactions are also influenced by watching and imitating those in our immediate environment, as filtered by our natural disposition (nurture and nature, respectively).

When it comes to personality-based responses, our natural disposition, nature, is just as important as the way we are socialized. Let's say, for example, a child with a very martial disposition grew up watching their father freeze in the face of danger. She may adopt the same-similar physical reaction, however, the internal happenings may be different. Whereas her father may have frozen in fear, literally paralyzed because his perception of the situation was too great to think about and act upon, she, being martial, might also physically freeze but mentally be strategizing to employ one of the other "f's," fight or flee.

As we move up in the psychoanalytical "hierarchy" of psychic forces, we encounter the Ego. Control of, and influence over, the Ego is the prize for which the Id and

Know thy self...

superego contend. A third contestant in this battle is the Ego itself. Every Ego strives for autonomy and would love to govern the life of its human host. You would think that the Ego had the superior advantage in this battle because it is its own prize and is fighting from within; unfortunately, this is not the case.

The process of gaining autonomy from, and assigning positions of influence and control to the Id and superego, is precisely what gives the Ego the experiences necessary for becoming and remaining sovereign and autonomous. Every fairytale and/or myth with a hero is based on the battle for the Ego. The "monster" every hero is seeking to slay (Agent Smith and his crew in *The Matrix*, Medusa and the other creatures in the Hercules tales, or The Joker and many other villains in the Batman series), is symbolic of their Id, and the wise woman or man (The Oracle in *The Matrix*, or Zeus in the story of Hercules, or Bruce Wayne's parents and his butler Alfred in the Batman series), is symbolic of the superego. The hero is the Ego.

Notice how in each of these stories, the hero has to ultimately struggle with their own issues before coming fully into power. And notice how this struggle is what actually provides the opportunity to realize their true power. These heroes are the individual egos claiming their freedom from emotional dictates, parental baggage projected onto them during childhood, the seemingly innate desire to covet and hoard, anxieties and fears, and the desires and repulsions harbored by the Id. Interestingly, each villain has already, or is currently undergoing the exact same process, ending with the final showdown between them and the hero. From the Villain's perspective, they are fighting society's expectation and dictate for them to be "good." They represent what Jung called "the shadow." Bruce Willis and Sam Jackson played this out in *Unbreakable*.

Some readers may remember "old school" cartoons

where the main character would find themselves in the middle of a cross-road situation, where a decision needs to be made. For example, Tom, from the *Tom & Jerry* cartoon, may be deciding whether or not to steal a pie from the windowsill, or Yakko might be faced with blowing up the *Warner Bros.* water tower in *Animaniacs*. In some instances, there would actually appear an "angel" and a "devil" above their left and right shoulders. The first clue to decipher the hidden meaning in this image is that both the "angel" and the "devil" are aspects of the character upon whose shoulders they stand. How do you know that Dr. Menzise? I'm glad you asked. This is evidenced by the fact that both the "angel" and the "devil" are miniature versions of the main character, dressed in white and red, respectively. The "angel" represents the superego, the "devil" represents the Id, and the main character, the Ego.

The word "Ego" literally translates into "I." This is the psychic structure that most people experience as their "self." It is the conscious aspect of the self, that makes decisions based on a variety of factors including impulses from the Id, and the sense of morality and wisdom provided by the Super Ego. The Ego, in its healthy state, is a conscious guardian over what is "allowed" to rise from the unconscious Id. It is like a gatekeeper, guarding something valuable. It is conscious expression, and represents the integrity of identity.

According to Western psychology, the Ego is said to begin forming during the first year of life, and consists of both the natural disposition as well as the socialized and conditioned aspects of the individual.[57] From the African-centered perspective, the Ego began with the initial separation of the personal and individual "soul" from God, during the initial act of creating humans, and is symbol-

---

57   You may have noticed the pattern of how almost all things in this respect are both nature and nurture, not either/or but and/both.

Know thy self...

ized as Ausar at the initial separation, then later as Heru once the conscious decision to live according to truth has been established.[58] The Ego is the decision maker, the executive manager, the monarch of your human experience. Just like each of these positions, the Ego receives council from various sources, including the Id and superego. The quality of the guidance depends heavily on the health of the Ego, and the programming and strength of both the Id and Super Ego.

Again, according to traditional African psychology, the Ego exists eternally, meaning it is intact prior to your birth. In fact, it was present prior to your conception, and will remain intact after your physical death. Some traditions say that the Ego eventually dissolves back into the source from which it came; other traditions maintain that it continues to "live" in another realm until eventually cycling back to the existence with which we are presently most familiar. It is the individualized (personalized) aspect of the infinite, which is also you.[59]

Part of the Ego's function is to prevent certain Id-based impulses from rising to the surface and being expressed, this is done through the *ego defense mechanisms.* Most ego defense mechanisms are unconscious, however, some, like *suppression,* may be carried out through a conscious and intentional process. This does not mean the behaviors and thoughts are unconscious, just that the motivation and desired outcomes are usually out of reach to the conscious mind. For example, self-sabotage because of self-doubt related to being ridiculed by a parent, may be motivated by the Ego's need to feel safe by staying in what is "comfortable." The fear and shame bubbles up from the unconscious, where the experience is stored, and subtly influences behavior.

---

58   In the Kemetic tradition
59   Some relate this to the Egyptian Ba and Ka.

Practical Psychology 101

As the fear and shame associated with the ridicule begins to surface, one of the ego defense mechanisms is then deployed to ensure that success is not obtained and therefore, things don't change. This, in turn, decreases the likelihood of being ridiculed for failing, because it has likely stopped the person from ever trying. This may play out by generating emotions, stimulating specific thoughts, and ensuring that certain perspectives are maintained, thereby influencing perception and stifling progress.

The covert nature of ego defense mechanisms is pretty slick, taking on ingenious forms. Think about your friend who always misses important appointments, or somehow seems to unintentionally squander opportunities that would likely lead to something great. Or how about the single relative that claims to be looking for love but somehow always ends up breaking up with a "good" person. The examples are endless, some of which will be shared as we further illustrate various other ego defense mechanisms.

Denial is a very popular and relatively easy to understand ego defense mechanism. This tool is activated when a person faces a fact of reality that is too difficult for their Ego to accept, respond, or react to, while at the same time maintaining its integrity. The Ego's integrity is usually directly related to social identity, the formation of which is based on how the person wants to be viewed by others, and how they would like to be in real life.

The following example should clearly illustrate the point. A person who finds out that their long-term business partner has been deceiving them regarding their contributions and the amount of money they were taking, will sometimes "refuse" to accept this reality by denying all evidence that may support the revelation. They'll come up with excuses and reasonings to maintain their disbelief. To an outsider, it may be plain that the situation is as it has

Know thy self...

been revealed to be, and supported by the evidence. To the Ego experiencing the drama of the situation, the evidence is "full of holes," be it: the "jealousy" of the messenger, or the "lack of credibility" of the source of information.

Richard Pryor illustrates this comically when he asked "You gonna believe me or your lying eyes?" in his classic joke about being caught, by his wife, in the act of cheating. In this example, Richard Pryor is playing on a person's need to avoid difficult situations and thus, he is trying to elicit a denial response. What we have here is a clear demonstration of psychology functioning as an active and practical tool; which is far from it being a passive subject for study, but instead, a science to be applied.

Another well known ego defense mechanism is *projection*. This tool activates when the person has difficulty dealing with aspects of his or her self that are deemed to be socially unacceptable and/or in conflict with the way a person would like to be viewed. Thus, as a protective measure, these traits and characteristics are super-imposed onto others. For example, a habitual liar will often accuse others of lying because, unconsciously, they may believe that lying is a negative trait and, perhaps, they really don't want to be known as a liar.

In this example, the Id, for whatever reason, has adopted lying as one of its methods for reacting to certain situations where the person feels they would suffer some sort of punishment or loss as a result of telling the truth. A person that constantly lies is likely unaware of the true motive behind their lies or that they are lying as often as they do. This is interesting because it means that the person may not be making a conscious decision to lie every time they tell a lie; however, they will rarely admit to the lie later, once they realize they have lied, or are in the process of lying. It's usually a knee-jerk reaction.

Continuing with projection, it is important to note

that characteristics of a society, or even those of an entire race and culture, can be projected onto other societies, races and cultures. For instance, the movie *Birth of a Nation* featured the depiction of an African man as the rapist of a White woman. During these times, from the initial invasion of the Americas by Europeans, up until the Reconstruction Era, rape was more likely to be carried out by White men and White women, with people of color being their victims. It's amazing because this irrational fear was actually experienced by some Whites, even though many knew that Africans and Native Americans were more likely to be raped by Whites, because they themselves had actually committed the atrocities. This example also serves as an illustration of how the definition of a "threat" is developed, programmed, and propagated.[60]

The many other ego defense mechanisms include, but are not limited to the following: *repression, sublimation, regression,* and *dissociation.* Each of these serve the purpose of protecting the Ego from facing an undesirable truth about itself, the people and/or environment, or certain experiences it is having or has had in the past. A thorough examination of each of these would prove fruitful, however, it goes beyond the scope of this particular manual.

As we can see, the Ego is very complex, powerful, and highly coveted by those seeking to control it (both internal and external forces). The external forces symbolically represent, and perhaps reflect the internal forces, and should be handled with as much care as one would their own internal processes. Complementary to the Id, the *Super Ego* serves as one of those internal factors that seeks to control the Ego, however for a different reason. While the Id seeks to fulfill desires and impulses related to basic needs, the superego is based on maintaining a sense of morality that relates to the individual's *ideal self,* and is

---

60   Refer back to the chapter on Learning.

Know thy self...

shaped by models in their environment, lessons from parents, religious teachings, and other revered sources. Some also believe the superego to be an internal and natural conscience, giving us a "pre-wired" sense of "right" and "wrong," that can be influenced and shaped.

The superego is thought to be developed, in part, through a process known as *identification*, which involves modeling and imitating desirable qualities and characteristics of a respected person or character. Keep in mind that this modeling and imitation is not a superficial mimicking, but a process of "becoming" that which is being imitated. It's an internalization of these attributes. There are varying degrees of identification, ranging from being inspired to do things in a similar fashion as the model, all the way to the point of obsessively taking on their personality and identity.[61] We see this in celebrity obsessions all the time.

The superego's job is to keep those impulses deemed "too embarrassing," or those that are in conflict with the person's sense of morality, from ever being openly expressed. It does this by informing and guiding the decisions of the Ego. Remember, the superego is the "angel" in our earlier example, softly whispering into the mind of the individual, trying to convince them to "do the right thing;" however that looks.

When society's examples and standards of morality are themselves lowly, questionable, and widespread, what you have is a lowering of the "moral IQ" of entire communities and cultures. This is problematic because the Id and superego are both competing for control of the Ego. If the moral aspect of the personality is in close alignment with the impulsive, need-fulfilling Id, you have a situation where the boundaries of what is acceptable are expanded and nothing seems to be sacred, leaving every sadistic and immoral desire to be openly played out with little to no

---

61   Chris Rock's character in CB4 is a perfect example.

remorse, regret, and hardly any socially imposed negative consequences. On the contrary, people may actually be rewarded by society at-large for their wayward, less-than-righteous behaviors, thoughts, and attitudes. This is exemplified by the "Enslavement-era" United States. Enslavers and plantation owners were proudly demonic, and heavily rewarded for being that way. Even men and women "of the cloth" participated without shame. In fact, they would actually bless the enterprise of enslavement in the name of their God.

This delicate balance between psychic forces is what becomes packaged as the personality. It becomes the set of characteristics used to define and identify a person. The personality becomes the baseline from which all other actions, thoughts, beliefs, and emotional reactions/responses are based. The saying that someone is "acting out of character," is saying that the observed behaviors are inconsistent with their personality, or at least what was thought to be their personality. You see this all the time when someone is caught committing a crime and a family member tells the news reporter that their nephew would never drive recklessly, so there is no way he was the "hit and run" driver; or that their niece was "always honest and upfront, if she was the one that broke the copier, she'd admit to it;" or how "granddad was the most generous person in the world, he'd never hide money from grandma."

There are countless numbers of real-world, real-time examples of how this phenomenon plays out in everyday life. Think of Charlottesville, VA, during the Summer 2017 protests, when the Ohio man drove into the crowd killing one person and injuring others. During a media interview, his mother stated that she was totally surprised by this behavior, and would have never expected this from her son. She also claimed to be ignorant of her son's political views or his identification as a White su-

Know thy self...

premacist.[62] Perhaps this is also an example of denial.

Again, these personality dispositions result from the interplay between the Id, Ego, and Super Ego. According to this perspective, if someone has a strong Id, they will likely be more impulsive, engage in risky behaviors, and perhaps present as less empathic regarding the feelings of others. A strong superego might make someone a worrier or a so-called prude. They may be what is stereotypically called a "holy roller," or someone who thinks they are "holier than thou," wearing their religion on their sleeve. A weak and insecure Ego is usually what gives way to being dominated by either of the other two psychic forces. According to psychoanalysts in agreement with Sigmund Freud, sexual energy is the motivating force or energy driving the entire process. This energy (*libido*) is known in other cultures as: *chi, qi, Ra, prana, kundalini,* etc.

Briefly, Freud's theory and stages of psychosexual development propose that the life force energy of human beings is driven by sexuality, which at its root, is a hard-wired drive for procreation and maintaining the species. Being conceived of sexual energy (sexual intercourse is how conception occurs, even if it is IVF or other mechanical forms of fertilization, it is still an imitation of sexual intercourse), it is thought that this same energy that propelled the ovum from the ovary, and the sperm from the testicles, continues and causes the embryo to grow, the fetus to develop, and the child to be born and to eventually transform into an adult.

The Id, Ego and Super Ego play a part in how Freud's five stages are negotiated, and thereby, deter-

---

62   One seemingly unrelated aspect of her interview, that struck me as curious, is the fact that she was somehow seated below the rear bumper of a vehicle during the interview about her son, using his vehicle as a weapon. Watch interview here: http://wtvr.com/2017/08/13/james-alex-fields-jr-mother-samantha-bloom-interview-charlottesville-rally-crowd/

mines how the personality is imprinted by the process. A child who develops during Freud's *oral stage*, overly dependent on oral stimulation for comfort, or who develops with very little gratification of necessary oral stimulation (not enough food to eat, mishandled teething, little to no healthy verbal communication), may develop an oral fixation which on a physical level manifests as seeking comfort by having something in their mouth (smoking objects, toothpicks, fingers, pens, chewing gum, etc.). They may also be verbally expressive to excess, or severely limited. Some also attribute the development of speech impediments, eating disorders, and even trouble with teeth, to issues arising during this stage of development.

A person with imbalances or issues rooted in Freud's *anal stage* of psychosexual development, may become what is known as an "anal retentive" person. This is thought to be related to how a person handled "potty training" as a child, based on their successes and failures, and how the people in their immediate environment responded and/or reacted to their ability or inability to not soil themselves. Issues at this stage can lead to an "obsessively" clean person or an incredibly messy individual. It can create a mind-state where every single detail matters, and matters a lot, or an individual that is carefree almost to a fault. The former are characteristics related to OCD (obsessive-compulsive disorder), and have been characterized by the lead detective in the television show, *Monk*.

Freud's other stages: *phallic, latency,* and *genital,* all have similar processes and a similar influence on personality characteristics. Like with most stage theories, how one stage is experienced will influence the outcomes and impact of later stages. It's like building a house, the foundation holds the rest up; if it is weak, the remainder of the structure is also weak based on its susceptibility to being compromised.

Know thy self...

Each phase has its core "conflict" needing to be resolved. For example, the phallic stage is known for the development of the *Elektra* and *Oedipal complexes*. The Elektra complex is when a female child has feelings of attraction towards the parent of the opposite sex, her father, and seeks to interfere with the intimate relationships he has with her mother. The Oedipal complex identifies when a male child has feelings of attraction for the mother and seeks to interfere with her intimate relationship with his father.

In both cases, the theory calls for the removal of the same sex parent, in order that they, the child, may "possess" the parent of the opposite sex. These feelings eventually give way to a more "rational" desire to identify with the same sex parent as opposed to getting rid of them. This dynamic is played out by "Stewie" of the animated sit-com *Family Guy*. There are other Freud related qualities of this show including the drawing of what appears to be phallic symbols on the faces of the main characters: the males seem to have a penis and testicles as their nose and chin, respectively; the female characters seem to have a clitoris and vaginal orifice as their nose and mouth, respectively.

Similarly, Erik Erikson saw the conflicts within various stages of development leading to the formation of our personalities. From his first stage, *Trust vs. Mistrust*, to his final stage, *Ego Integrity vs. Despair*, Erikson saw value in environmental interactions for their powerful influence over personality development. These factors gradually go from being physically-based to a more philosophical orientation. The earlier stages (*trust vs. mistrust, autonomy vs. shame and doubt, industry vs. inferiority*) serve as the foundation upon which *ego identity* stands. If the person developed as a mistrusting and shameful individual, suffering from an unresolved inferiority complex and self-esteem issues, their ego identity will reflect this in adolescence.

This ego identity, as the opposite one that develops as a trusting, autonomous and motivated, confident, self-starter, is what shapes the young adult as they grow to the elder stages of life. The negatively slanted ego identity is more likely to be without sincere intimate relationships, less likely to feel fulfilled in their professional endeavors, and will likely be upset when reflecting on their lives near its end. The positive ego identity is more likely to have secure intimate relationships, develop with a sense of being fulfilled in their accomplishments, and will likely be satisfied as they review their life and accomplishments.

Erikson demonstrated how, from this perspective, racism helped to shape and mold both the perception and reality of American African personality and identity development. In his words:

> But what if the "milieu" is determined to let live only at the expense of a permanent loss of identity?
>
> Consider, for example, the chances for a continuity of identity in the American Negro child. I know a colored boy who, like our boys, listens every night to Red Rider. Then he sits up in bed, imagining that he is Red Rider. But the moment comes when he sees himself galloping after some masked offenders and suddenly notices that in his fancy Red Rider is a colored man. He stops his fantasy. While a small child, this boy was extremely expressive, both in his pleasures and in his sorrows. Today he is calm and always smiles; his language is soft and blurred; nobody can hurry him or worry him—or please him. White people like him.
>
> Negro babies often receive sensual satisfactions which provide them with enough oral and sensory surplus for a lifetime, as clearly betrayed in the way they move, laugh, talk, sing. Their forced symbiosis with the feudal South capitalized on this oral-sensory treasure and helped to build a slave's

Know thy self...

identity: mild, submissive, dependent, somewhat querulous, but always ready to serve, with occasional empathy and childlike wisdom. But underneath a dangerous split occurred. The Negro's unavoidable identification with the dominant race, and the need of the master race to protect its own identity against the very sensual and oral temptations emanating from the race held to be inferior (whence came their mammies), established in both groups an association: light—clean—clever—white, and dark—dirty—dumb—nigger. The result, especially in those Negroes who left sudden and cruel cleanliness training, as attested to in the autobiographies of Negro writers. It is as if by cleansing, a whiter identity could be achieved. The attending disillusionment transmits itself to the phallic-locomotor stage, when restrictions as to what shade of girl one may dream of interfere with the free transfer of the original narcissistic sensuality to the genital sphere. Three identities are formed: (1) mammy's oral-sensual "honey-child"—tender, expressive, rhythmical; (2) the evil identity of the dirty, anal-sadistic, phallic-rapist "nigger"; and (3) the clean, anal-compulsive, restrained, friendly, but always sad "white man's Negro."

So-called opportunities offered the migrating Negro often only turn out to be a more subtly restricted prison which endangers his only historically successful identity (that of the slave) and fails to provide a reintegration of the other identity fragments mentioned. These fragments, then, become dominant in the form of racial caricatures which are underscored and stereotyped by the entertainment industry. Tired of his own caricature, the colored individual often retires into hypochondriac invalidism as a condition which represents an analogy to the dependence and the relative safety of defined restrictions in the South: a neurotic regression to the ego identity of the slave.

I have mentioned the fact that mixed-blood Indians in areas where they hardly ever see Negroes refer to their full-blood brothers as "niggers," thus indicating the power of the dominant national

Practical Psychology 101

imagery which serves to counterpoint the ideal and the evil images in the inventory of available prototypes. No individual can escape this opposition of images, which is all-pervasive in the men and in the women, in the majorities and in the minorities, and in all the classes of a given national or cultural unit. Psychoanalysis shows that the unconscious evil identity (the composite of everything which arouses negative identification—i.e., the wish not to resemble it) consists of the images of the violated (castrated) body, the ethnic outgroup, and the exploited minority. Thus a pronounced he-man may, in his dreams and prejudices prove to be mortally afraid of ever displaying a woman's sentiments, a Negro's submissiveness, or a Jew's intellectuality. For the Ego, in the course of its synthesizing efforts, attempts to subsume the most powerful evil and ideal prototypes (the final contestants as it were) and with them the whole existing imagery of superior and inferior, good and bad, masculine and feminine, free and slave, potent and impotent, beautiful and ugly, fast and slow, tall and small, in a simple alternative, in order to make one battle and one strategy out of a bewildering number of skirmishes...

The Negro, of course, is only the most flagrant case of an American minority which by the pressure of tradition and the limitation of opportunity is forced to identify with its own evil identity fragments, thus jeopardizing whatever participation in an American identity it may have earned. —

Childhood and Society, Erik Erikson, pp 241 - 243

This perspective and reality gave way to the various characteristics of Black identity and personality development as detailed by Black/African personality theorist listed earlier in this chapter. African/Black personality is often expressed as an unhealthy personality driven by reactions to the psychopathic racial personalities of those perpetuating racism/White supremacy; fueling a drive to survive by any necessary means, even if it means intentionally developing in unhealthy ways, along the

Know thy self...

various stage conflicts listed by Erikson, manifesting as issues found within each of Freud's psycho-sexual stages, or perhaps more relevant, manifesting as the pathologies of personality identified by Akbar (*alien-self* and *anti-self disorders*) or proposed by Bobby Wright (*mentacide*).

The last personality perspective we will explore, derived from the psychoanalytical approach, is based on Jung's four principal psychological functions: *sensation, intuition, feeling,* and *thinking*. Based on the combination of a specific configuration of these traits, a profile is formed that identifies a person's strengths and weaknesses, aversions, preferences, tendencies, and dispositions. A very popular assessment tool used to generate this profile is the *Myers-Briggs Type Indicator* (*MBTI*). Theoretically, how a person scores on this test, identifies certain characteristics and traits of their personality. This is definitely not the strongest personality measure, regardless of how popular and widely used it is. Nonetheless, it does serve a purpose and provides guidance for those who need data related to personality and predicting human behavior.

On the other end of the personality conversation is the *trait* perspective, which is not mutually exclusive from the psychoanalytical perspective, but diverges enough to warrant its own category. The psychoanalytical perspective and trait perspectives share many common variables, differing mostly on the proposed origins of these variables and how they are shaped. Traits, regardless of their theoretical origins, are *relatively stable characteristics of personality that are determined by observing behaviors*. An "outgoing" person is said to be so based on self-report and observations. They are expected to consistently be this way, to one degree or another, across situation and context. It is the same for people considered to be mean, gullible, ignorant, ratchet, peaceful, etc.

Many personality theorists have contributed greatly to the trait perspective of personality including: Jung (although a psychoanalyst, he is cited as the first to draw a distinction between introverts and extroverts), Robert McCrae, and Paul T. Costa, Jr.

The latter two theorists, McCrae and Costa, Jr., are known for their work towards developing the *Five-Factor Model* of personality, a trait theory that presents an understanding of personality as it relates to five basic factors: *extraversion, neuroticism, conscientiousness, agreeableness,* and *openness to experience.* Each of these characteristics are measured on a continuum, identifying the two extremes of each trait. People are then given a profile describing how engaging they are, ranging from passive to assertive; how likable they are, from kind to hostile; how considerate of others they are, ranging from thoughtful to negligent; how calm they are, ranging from excessively nervous and moody, to adaptable and being able to cope with ease; and finally how flexible their minds are, ranging from imaginative, creative and curious, to shallow, close-minded, and lacking in awareness.

Moving along, we come to Hippocrates' personality types which are based on the *four humors* or body fluids, all of which have very unique characteristics and were once thought to influence personality. The four humors are: *blood, yellow bile, black bile,* and *phlegm.* Each humor is associated with the following personality types, respectively: *sanguine, choleric, melancholic,* and *phlegmatic.* This, and the psychoanalytical perspectives, are the two Western psychological perspectives that resonate most closely with an African-centered conceptualization of personality. This is not surprising when we consider that both the Greeks (Hippocrates' kinfolk) and psychoanalysts Freud & Jung, both studied African philosophy, spirituality, and science.[63]

According to Hippocrates' version, these person-

---

63   See, *Jung in Africa (2005)* by Blake Wiley Burleson

Know thy self...

ality dispositions are all based on the balance and condition of the four humors within the body. Depending on which of the humors is in balance, in excess, or depleted, and of good or poor quality, is the individual's susceptibility to certain medical and psychological strengths and disorders.[64] For example, the choleric personality can be optimistic and active in their healthy and balanced state, and aggressive, impulsive, and restless in the negative state. Sanguine individuals can be outgoing, sociable, great in diplomatic endeavors; while in an unbalanced state, they can be scheming, disloyal, and unreliable. The melancholic person in a balanced state can be stable, dependable, thoughtful, strategic and calculated; on the unbalanced extreme, they are prone to depression, pessimism, fickleness, being withdrawn, isolated and non-social. The phlegmatic personality is reliable, calm, and easy going in its healthy state, on the negative extreme it can manifest as congestion, stagnation, indecisiveness, and lacking in both structure and self-control.

In some ancient African perspectives of personality, these four humors manifest as four elements: fire, air, water, and earth. According to Malidoma Some', the Dagara in Burkino Faso, West Africa, additionally consider the element of metal (this is consistent with Traditional Chinese Medicine and philosophy, which also includes wood). Just like the four humors, these elements are symbolic of certain characteristics, qualities, and temperaments. This symbolism is firmly rooted in the reality of nature, and is a genius way to classify and categorize all of creation, including humans and their personalities.

According to this African-centered perspective, each element manifests as the product of humidity interacting with temperature. As you can see in the chart below, four quadrants are formed identifying the product of the

---

64   This is similar to Traditional Chinese Medicine.

different extremes, for both temperature and humidity. On the vertical axis, you have temperature represented by H (hot) and C (cool), and the horizontal axis representing humidity as M (moist) and D (dry).

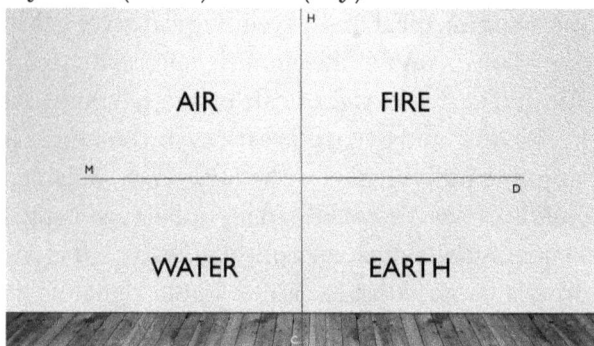

Fire is the configuration of hot and dry; Water is cold and moist; Air is hot and moist; Earth is cold and dry. In the Kemetic (Ancient Egyptian) creation stories, this interaction is often detailed by the interactions of Shu, Tefnut, Ra, Geb, and Nut. From these configurations are spawned all things in creation, which is why every single thing or combination of things you could possibly think of, fits nicely into one of these element-based categories. This represents the Omnipresence, and thus, Omnipotence and Omniscience of God. Think about it, if something is *IN* all things, and *IS* all things, then It is everywhere, and knows everything, individually, collectively, simultaneously and at different points in time; therefore it can *DO* all things.

It is very important for us to understand that within each element-quadrant, there are an infinite number of points, each identifying a varying degree of each element in that particular quadrant (combination of temperature and humidity). This information helps to illustrate the fact that there are infinite numbers of individual personality "types," while being only four main categories for expression (air, earth, fire, water). With each of the following examples, try to draw a correlation between the examples

Know thy self...

found in broader nature, and those found in the nature of human beings; you'll see they are one and the same.

In the earth quadrant, we can see the various manifestations of earth by adjusting the amount of moisture and temperature. Extremely hot and dry earth is sand. Extremely hot and moist earth is lava. Extremely cold and dry earth is metal or rock. Extremely cold and moist earth is the frozen land found under and within glaciers of ice. These are the extremes, with all points in between being represented within the quadrant. Let's take a look at the other elements.

The fire quadrant has variations as well. We will first look at how fire varies in moisture. An example of a moist fire is illustrated by a camp fire. The wood offers its moisture to the fire, giving the fire a sense of fluidity as it dances atop the wood. These fires are slow to start (depending on the moisture in the wood) and often are long lasting once they get started; giving off a different kind of smoke. An extremely dry fire is represented by lightning or electricity. It burns at intense temperatures and is very short-lived and can be erratic and "destructive" in nature. On the temperature side, we typically have distinctions in the "quantity" of fire present. This is measured in *BTUs* (*British* or *Bio Thermal Units*), degrees on a thermometer, or in *Joules, Calories,* and *Watts.* These measurements usually refer to the amount of work the heat performs,[65] whether that's in the form of changing the temperature of water (calories) or the rate of heat transfer (watts). Hotter fire is usually more fire (my Rastafarian friends will see what I did here), while the cooler fire is easily represented by a single match. This is tricky because touching the head of a burning match, or simply measuring its temperature, you will find that it too is extremely hot (600 to 800

---

65   This is paradoxical because typically "heat" is contrasted with "work" in the field of thermodynamics.

degrees), yet it does not do much to warm an environment on its own. A single candle burns anywhere between 600 and 1400 degrees, but again, you'd be hard pressed to change the temperature of a small room using the fire of a single wick. Contrast this with the temperature changing potential of the sun or a flame thrower. One of the interesting traits of fire is how easily it transfers its energy to other things; this is where the power held within a candle and single match resides.

The single match can transfer its heat generating potential to other matches, to wood, to paper, to cotton, and other combustible sources of "fuel," thereby increasing the temperature and activated potential of that fire. This was recently illustrated by the two teenagers, mentioned earlier, who are allegedly responsible for the forest fire that ravaged Gatlinburg, Tennessee. Although witnesses claim to have observed the pair lighting and throwing matches along the trails, all charges were dropped.

As temperature increases, the molecules making up the heated material, and the air around it, begin to move at a quicker rate and in more erratic patterns. This is why ice does not usually move on its own accord, and definitely not easily. However, once the ice is heated and begins to melt, it will begin to slide on its self-produced stream of water. As it becomes totally liquid (water), the molecules are far more expansive and easier to manipulate and move, than when they were solid. As we continue to increase the temperature, the molecules move faster and even more erratically, until eventually, it changes state once again, going from liquid to gas. This is done by the molecules freeing themselves from each other, evaporating into steam (moist air), thereby becoming a gas.

In the above paragraph, we have intentionally crossed over into our next category: air. Air has a base configuration of hot and moist. The variation of tempera-

Know thy self...

ture and moisture in air is best illustrated by experiencing air in various environments and in various contexts. Imagine air found in a tropical rain forest, compared to the air found in the basement of an old house. It has a different smell, and feel to it. Imagine the feeling of air after a summer rain shower, when it's ninety degrees outside; now contrast that with the air in the Sahara desert. Or how the air quality after a snow storm is much different than air during a heat wave, or the stifling heat of your city's housing projects in the middle of July...very little moisture and very little movement of the air. This is the reason why dry air feels more difficult to breath—moisture is required for movement.

These descriptions are very basic for each of the elements and can be expanded almost infinitely. The genius of the African classification of reality based on nature and the elements is, as mentioned above, the ability to easily transfer this insight to people, animals, insects, foods, and even social situations. You will find a complete detailing of these interactions in the various mythologies of the many cultures of Africa. In Egypt, in the Kemetic mythology, you will find these told in the stories of the Puat Neteru. In Nigeria and Yoruba lore, you will find it spelled out by the characters of the Orisha and their interactions. This is pure genius, especially when we gain a thorough understanding of how these personified manifestations of temperature interacting with humidity, are actually profiles of the various human personalities.

The following quote from the Greek text, *Kore Kosmou* (*Virgin of the World*), credited to Hermes Trismegistus (a Greek variation of the Ancient African principle of Wisdom - Tehuti/Djehuti/Thoth), illustrates this knowledge of psychology held by the Africans of the Nile Valley. This is where the personality constructs attributed to Hippocrates earlier in this chapter, actually come from.

Practical Psychology 101

And Isis answer made: Of living things, my son,
some are made friends with fire, and some with
water, some with air, and some with earth, and some
with two or three of these, and some with all. And,
on the contrary, again some are made enemies of
fire, and some of water, some of earth, and some of
air, and some of two of them, and some of three, and
some of all. For instance, son, the locust and all flies
flee fire; the eagle and the hawk and all high-flying
birds flee water; fish, air and earth; the snake avoids
the open air. Whereas snakes and all creeping things
love earth; all swimming things love water; winged
things, air, of which they are the citizens; while those
that fly still higher love the fire and have the habitat
near it. Not that some of the animals as well do not
love fire; for instance salamanders, for they even
have their homes in it. It is because one or another of
the elements doth form their bodies' outer enve-
lope. Each soul, accordingly, while it is in its body is
weighted and constricted by these four.

Marinating in the beauty of this wisdom, meta-
phorically being passed along from Mother (Auset/Isis) to
Son (Heru/Horus), is an initiation in and of itself. It is the
method by which we begin to strengthen and develop the
various aspects and tools of our personalities. This is the
mystery encoded in the symbols of humans with animal
heads found throughout the Kemetic symbology. The animal heads represents very specific mental attributes that
are awakened and in use in that moment. These personality configurations have been well preserved in the zodiacs
of the Western world and can be found in an earlier form
in the Temple of Denderah in Egypt. Notice that animals
are used to identify these various zones of heavenly influence as well. By relating each of the characters found
amongst the Kemetic Neteru, or the Yoruba Orisha, or the
Haitian Lwa, or the Saints of Santeria, to an element, we
can see the science of personality at work from an astronomical, astrological, and culturally speaking, an African

Know thy self...

spiritual perspective. With this in mind, we will briefly revisit Freud's discussion of the three psychic forces competing for dominance over the psychological expression of humans, as a key to understanding personality.

Our point of reference for this exploration is the *Tree of Life* as detailed by Ra Un Nefer Amen in his *Metu Neter* series. As you will find in Vol. 1, each of the Neteru has a direct correlation with an Orisha of the Ifa tradition. There are Neteru that correlate with each of the four elements (air, earth, fire, water), just like there are air, earth, fire, and water signs of the zodiac. Additionally, there are Neteru that correlate more closely with the functioning of one of Freud's three psychic forces (Id, Ego, Super Ego), and interestingly, each Neter also has manifestations that identify which of the psychic forces is dominant. Amen categorized them as Ba, Ab, and Sahu, which I correlate with the Super Ego, Ego, and Id, respectively. The Ba correlates with the divine aspect of human beingness; the Ab is the seat of humanity, identity and self-expression; and the Sahu is the basic physiological, emotional, and brain-based cognitive functioning of the person.

Much like the modern psychological assessment tools, spiritual tools are used in the various divination systems found around the world to identify "personality types," as well as many other psychological and cognitive attributes. In the Yoruba tradition, qualified practitioners (priests and priestesses) employ divination tools to identify which of the Orisha "rules the person's head," meaning which one is the dominant force in their personality, ultimately governing their life experiences and their destiny. Other cultures use various versions of astronomical configurations to do the same, this is the field of astrology.

Many African-centered personality theorists and scholars have worked to translate ancient worldview science into information that is applicable to our modern needs and understandings. Amongst these are Kobi Kambon, Bobby Wright, Ra Un Nefer Amen, Linda James Myers, Na'im Akbar, and Amos Wilson. Each of them have put forth theories and/or perspectives of African personality that are universally valuable to anyone interested in better understanding the fullness of human nature. This information is equally valuable, as we will soon see, to organizers and front-line activists.

A little later in this chapter, we will refer back to the Kemetic "Tree of Life" as detailed by Ra Un Nefer Amen, listing 11 basic "personality types" personified as Neteru. Keep in mind that these African personality types are actually the various aspects and/or tools concealed within the personality of everyone and everything. Many of us are limited in our ability to fully express the various aspects of our personality because we tend to singularly focus on the dominant energy, claiming that bit to be the whole. The degree to which these can be consciously, consistently, and appropriately employed, in a variety of situations and circumstances, depicts the level of self-mastery and situational awareness obtained by the person.

Before we list these types, let's make this a bit more plain. The individual with a fiery, martial disposition, is typically high energy, perhaps impulsive, fearless and/or reckless, may be quick to fight, prone to dangerous situations, thrill-seeking behaviors, and may easily put their life on the line for others. This individual may encounter a situation in which it is most beneficial for them to lay low, and perhaps become "invisible." In this case, they'd need to take on the qualities of air, which is only noticeable by its impact on other things. Air is also evasive, meaning it is very hard to "capture," although it is pretty easy to direct and channel, thereby harnessing its energy. Becoming air in a "fight" situation may manifest as being able to

Know thy self...

talk your way out of a physical altercation,[66] or to harness the "jab-slipping" abilities of a Muhammed Ali or a Floyd Mayweather.

The same person with a martial disposition may need to become earth in a situation, meaning they are solid and needing to stand their ground, becoming immovable both by external (threats from others) and internal forces (emotions and mental perceptions). Because fire and water are "opposites" in regards to elements, they have a point of intersection while simultaneously being furthest apart from each other. Think about how fire and water interact in the natural world. It is almost impossible for them to interact directly without changing; they always require some sort of mediator to maintain their integrity.

This mediator is the pot used to boil the water. It literally touches both the fire and the water, allowing for the fire to transfer its energy through the metal surface (earth) in order for it to interact with the water without the risk of being extinguished by the extreme moisture of water. Just imagine the volatile reaction fire has when someone pours water onto it. It almost erupts into steam. There is enough power released in this interaction that entire trains (steam engines) are operated simply by creating this condition and harnessing the energy. Bruce Lee, a martial artist, advised us to "be like water." Fela tells us that *Water No Get No Enemy*. Both are advising how to avoid or at least control potentially adverse fire situations through the use of water. This places our attitudes and dispositions as the locus of control for our experiences.

Understanding what we have discussed thus far is necessary for applying this knowledge to your political and social activism. The active and intentional use of personality types to assign roles and tasks to members of an organization is the master key to efficiency and effectiveness, as

---

66   Remember verbal communication aligns with the air element

Practical Psychology 101

long as each category is allowed to function autonomously within its own area of expertise, without being hindered by someone who does not understand those categories, and who has not developed them within their own personality. The *Divergent* movie series is an excellent illustration of this point. The factions that children are placed into, is based on their personality types. You can see it clearly by how they move and the sort of activities they are drawn toward. The *Avatar* cartoon series is also a great example.

This is where many organizations fail; having leadership that has not evolved in their own personality to the point of mastery of the four elements (which is recognized by their ability to present from any of the four elements, at will, and according to an accurate assessment of the situation at hand). Organizations are often troubled by the squandering of their human resources, and by not capitalizing on the natural gifts and talents that a person may possess by virtue of their natural disposition. This opportunity is often opposed by the arbitrary placement of people into a role that does not fit their natural disposition, and/or their level of mastery.

The Ausar Auset Society is a wonderful, real-world example of how an organization properly utilizes this knowledge for its own benefit. Members are grouped based on their *moon sign* into "Clans" governed by the re-lated Neteru. Each Clan contributes to the whole from its members' natural dispositions and developed abilities.

The other benefit gained from applying this knowl-edge to activism is the ability to correctly read the "ener-gy" of other people and situations. The political activist participating in a protest, counter-protest, demonstration, or some other form of public expression, is benefited by their ability to "read" the environment and pick up on the subtle cues of the people and things surrounding them. In Charlottesville, VA, some protesters seemed to have been

Know thy self...

caught off guard by the sudden and seemingly sporadic eruptions of violence. Those that were ran over by the suspected White supremacist from Ohio, may have missed the imminent danger "vibe" that must have been projected into the environment as the driver decided to attempt mass murder using his vehicle as the weapon. There were others who felt the threat, and got out the way, pushed others out of the way, or somehow, perhaps instinctively, made a decision to go down another street altogether. In middle school, I had the experience of one of these precognitions.

There was a basketball game taking place in our gym one evening. My friends and I were all planning to attend. I got a feeling as the school day came close to an end, telling me it was not a good idea to stay after school for the basketball game. I had no concrete evidence to substantiate this feeling, nonetheless, I felt sure that it would be dangerous to ignore the "advice" I had received. I began to tell my friends not to go to the game. Naturally, they asked "Why?" And of course, I said, "I don't know. I just have a feeling that we shouldn't go." They went, I didn't.

The next day at school, some folks had black eyes and "speed knots,"[67] while others were absent from school altogether. I later learned that some people from the neighborhood decided, for whatever reason, to come to the gym with bats, chains, and sticks, and literally started kicking butt; I mean they ROLLED on our school.[68]

---

67   A term made popular by the hip hop legend Redman in his song "Sooperman Luva." He used the term in reference to the observable lumps on someone's face after a fight where they weren't quick enough to dodge the punches. Like that *Martin* episode when he fought Tommy "The Hitman" Hearns. https://www.youtube.com/watch?v=F-NBkFsiCK9w&feature=youtu.be

68   Lucky for us, we had weekly, if not daily, "fight clubs" in the form of class-wars. This was a phenomenon where groups of people from various graduating classes: Nine-one (c/o 1991), Nine-four (c/o 1994), Nine-five (c/o 1995), would literally square off with each other and have a brawl on an outside, concrete pavilion. People must've

Practical Psychology 101

Knowing what I now know about the workings of situational awareness, energy, and being able to accurately read it, I am pretty sure that the flash of intuition I received as a "feeling," likely occurred at the very moment the plan to come to the school was solidified by the neighborhood crew; thereby changing the energy of the basketball game that was yet to happen. As you may have noticed, this example demonstrates how consciousness overlaps with personality. As previously stated, each of the areas discussed throughout this manual are interrelated, interdependent, and simultaneously exist as an independent area for study.

Had I been an organizer at my school, I could have taken this insight and organized my friends in such a way that they could have avoided the approaching danger. Had I been part of an organized group wherein we understood the power of identifying and recognizing personality, I may have been identified as one of the members who had great insight, intuition, and perhaps psychic abilities (or simply a keen sense of perception), and my warnings would have been trusted and followed by those in my circle. Without this knowledge, and the lack of an intentionally organized group, the outcome was what it was.

Viewing Amen's "Tree of Life" diagram (below) as a blueprint for personality types, provides an excellent reference for those interested in making knowledge of personality practical. As mentioned, it provides a readily accessible categorization of personality in the form of the personified Neteru. Each Neteru, represented by the eleven spheres, can be placed within one of the four quadrants of the element chart, and is also easily correlates with one of the psychic forces presented by Freud.

Below is a brief listing of the characteristics associated with the 11 personality types that correlate with each

---

thought we were soft because we were a "magnet school," I guess.

Know thy self...

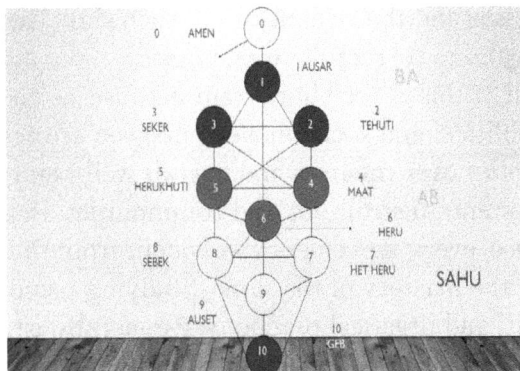

Neteru (for more details, see Ra Un Nefer Amen's Metu Neter, vols. 1 & 2):

> **Amen** - peace, emotional and mental calmness
> **Ausar** - lack of conditionings, universal, adaptable
> **Tehuti** - wise, insightful, knowledgeable
> **Seker** - deep thinker, structured, organized, slow to make decision, stubborn, stable, steady, dependable
> **Maat** - diplomatic, group oriented, generous, networker, organizer, can see the forest and the trees
> **Herukhuti** - martial, fearless, impulsive, strong, disciplined, reckless, erratic, focused, withdrawn
> **Heru** - circumspect, insightful, clarity of vision, leadership skills, arrogant, confident
> **Het Heru** - aesthetically pleasing, social, fun, sensual, harmonious, sweet
> **Sebek** - talkative, loquacious vocabulary, tricky, funny, persuasive, informed, thinker
> **Auset** - nurturing, educator, healer, compassionate, devoted, loving, motherly, dependable, dedicated, receptive, insightful
> **Geb** - interested in healing concepts, wealth/resources, solidity, stability, structures

See if you can recognize yourself, and your own disposition in any of these descriptions. It is likely that you will have an affinity for more than one, but one more than others. See if these same characteristics also align with your zodiac sign (sidereal or vedic, not tropical). Identify the strengths and the weaknesses of each sign, then use the strengths to correct the weaknesses.

All of this is very important because, as an organizer of political and social movements, you are accepting responsibility over the lives and overall well-being of people, systems, institutions and communities. Regardless of the cause, every movement can benefit from this knowledge, and the mastery of the same. Studying personality specifically, and practical psychology generally, grants benefits that are directly translatable into efficiency, effectiveness, and success. It will help you to better understand the enemy that you face, and how that relates to your own personality dispositions, strengths and weaknesses.

As stated in Ancient Greek and Egyptian philosophies, you should "Know Thyself in Order to Know God." This means to get to know your person to the point of mastery, because by doing so, you are more likely to also gain mastery and dominion over all other things (Omniscience, Omnipresence, and Omnipotence).

Mastering personalities, yours or someone else's, whether as a leader or a member of a group, will invariably provide you with the tools necessary to make the most out of your participation. This will simultaneously empower you with the tools you'll need to survive and thrive, both on the frontline, and in life in general. It has been a longtime belief that knowledge of self is the highest form of knowledge one could gain. Who are you?

Chapter 8
Going forward...

Psychology, the study of the soul, is perhaps one of the most important subjects to learn and master. Regardless of your professional, religious, social, political, and personal interest, a strong command of psychologically-based information will only serve to benefit and enhance your overall life experience. Beyond having information, being able to understand and apply various aspects of psychology to the many areas of your life will grant you a degree of self-mastery that may otherwise be unknown.

Of all the practical sciences, psychology is the one to most readily illustrate how all things in creation are interrelated, to one degree or another. Yes, you can find evidence in biology via the interrelationships between the mineral, plant, and animal kingdoms. Of course it is made plain by the laws of physics, which are equally applicable to all things in the known universe (whether we can understand this application is a separate issue). There is not a person capable of denying chemistry's offering that all matter is made of the same substance, and undergoes change in a manner unique to its kind. Despite these facts, it is psychology that shows us how each of these disciplines rely on the capabilities of humans to perceive, comprehend, think (deductively and inductively), and even manipulate the substance of these disciplines in order that they may be known. In fact, without psychology, there is little to no understanding of the known knower.

Practical Psychology 101

Psychology is that bridge linking all things via human beings. It is a discipline that informs the majority of today's industries; in fact, it's because of psychology that every industry exists, and thrives or decays. Without knowledge of how human beings function, on a mental and psychological level, we would be forced to rely solely on the mechanistic aspects of human behavior. We would have no need for the theological sciences. There would be no place for sociology, no role for marketing, and anthropology & archaeology would become glorified play-dates in the deserted sandboxes of history.

Because psychology is based on the worldview and cultural orientation of the world's people, we will find that the soul is defined and explored differently amongst them. This is important because this definition ultimately informs what we are looking for, why we are looking at and for it, and how we go about doing these things. It informs what we believe the soul is, how it functions, and the role it plays in day-to-day living. For cultures that carry as a main belief the non-existence of the soul, it makes sense that there will likely not be a method for utilizing it; therefore, they forfeit all the benefits that come with consciously studying the soul.[69]

For the cultures placing the soul at the highest aspect of human beingness, meaning it is superior and more valuable than the physical, mental, and psychic aspects of our nature, we may find a neglect of physical reality in exchange for a greatly enhanced mental, emotional, spiritual and social experience. These cultures are typically non-materialistic, live communally, and hold as their highest value, the peaceful interaction between and amongst people and nature. Social harmony, as established

---

69   I say consciously because there are aspects of the soul/psychology that operate regardless of an individual's belief and/or knowledge of its existence.

Going forward...

by humans who intentionally maintain the intrinsic balance between their internal and external nature, is what all systems in such a society are based upon; the degree to which these systems fall in line or out of sync, determines the health and well being of everything within the system.

This is also true for those cultures that place the soul in equilibrium with the other aspects of human being-ness. This perspective understands that the soul is just as important as the physical, emotional, psychic, social, and other aspects of personhood. These societies are built on systems that seek to holistically develop its people, civilization, and culture; understanding that each one influences the others. For example, physical health, directly influences one's mental capacities, just as one's mental capacities directly impacts their physical condition. This is evidenced by hunger's effect on a person's thinking capacity, emotional state, and behaviors (ex. folks getting "hangry.").

Further evidence is shown by the person who systematically endures a fast, giving up some form of eating/ ingesting. These people often report a clarity of mind and increased levels of productivity. Or how the loss of function in one physical sense, often develops a keener performance of another sense. And how a person's emotional state is known to impact decision making, behaviors, and so on. Perhaps the most profound example of the relationship between the mind and body is that of the so-called "placebo effect." This is when a person is given a sugar pill, a saline solution, or a "fake" surgery, all the while believing they are being treated for an ailment, and actually show psychologically and physiologically-measurable signs of improvement. Western medicine rarely explains how this operates, although they will note that it does take place. You can find more details about these instances under the label of *spontaneous remission*.[70]

---

70   The Institute for Noetic Science has documented over 3500

Practical Psychology 101

Cultures that balance mind, body and spirit, often have systems of education and socialization designed to strengthen each and every aspect of the developing person, giving intellectual and academic development its place alongside the development of trades, emotional intelligence, social mastery, and spiritual empowerment. They are often more interested in well-developed humans than they are interested in amassing physical possessions; their number one natural resource is the holistically-viewed human being. Another important, yet unfortunate similarity held amongst these cultures is the fact that they typically have also been attacked and conquered by those who place the highest value on physical domination, and measure progress by their ability to identify and collect resources and people to control.

All of this is important as it relates to social justice movements because, as mentioned before, we are always dealing with people and people come in all forms, with all kinds of baggage, and with all kinds of capabilities, disabilities, and other means of functioning. To know as much as possible about these varieties, and to be able to recognize and masterfully engage these variations, will place you beyond experiences that catch you by surprise and ill-prepared. Showing up the best version of you, to any situation, relies heavily on your ability to show up knowledgeable about human psychology, with self-mastery as your prime objective.

Up to this point, we have provided an overview of various aspects of psychology from both the Modern/Western perspective, as well as the more Ancient/Eastern holistic perspectives. In addition to providing definitions and background information on each topic, we have also highlighted their utility as tools for navigating social jus-

cases of spontaneous remission. http://noetic.org/research/projects/spontaneous-remission

Going forward...

tice movements, demonstrations, protests, and your day-to-day life experiences. Having this knowledge and seeking to understand and apply it to your life should be high upon the "to-do list" of anyone seeking to organize and/or join a movement centered on social justice. It both decreases one's susceptibility to negative and unwanted influences, while making them more stable, empowered, and effective as an activist.

By now, you should feel equipped with a perspective that at least includes a broader and deeper respect for psychology, its importance as a subject of study, and as a science for practical application. Each chapter has jewels that can be mined, polished, and even restructured to form a powerful position from which to launch into any activity involving human behavior. These jewels are applicable to all aspects of people activity including, but not limited to: economics, entertainment, education, labor, law, politics, religion, sex, and war/counter-war. It's up to you, the reader, to take the next steps of internalizing and applying them.

The following quote by revolutionary educator, and master teacher Asa Hilliard helps to summarize and contextualize the motivation behind this manual, and hopefully will inspire and give further direction to you, as you set out to do this important work of fighting for social justice.

> ...as long as there has been both privilege and oppression, there has also been agitation and activity against them. During slavery, there was the abolitionist movement. During the period of segregation, there was the desegregation movement. Since 1954, the year of the Supreme Court decision outlawing school segregation, Brown v. Topeka Board of Education, many different types of activities by many different individuals, agencies, and groups have been initiated to deal in one way or another with some aspect of equity. These include affirmative

Practical Psychology 101

action programs in hiring, human relations training programs, multicultural education staff development programs, equal opportunity programs funded by the federal government, and legal assistance and class action suits on behalf of oppressed groups. Therefore, we may say that the problem has never existed in the absence of activity.

In my opinion, the more serious problem is the absence of comprehensive and rational planning to make these various activities more efficient and effective.

Thousands of citizens from all walks of life have engaged in remedial activities, but no one has yet developed a clear conceptual base and theoretical framework from which to operate. At this point, we stand at a crossroad where we can choose either to continue the "ad hocracy"[71] of practice or to undertake the difficult conceptual work that, if done well, can result in significant improvements...

- *"Conceptual Confusion and the Persistence of Group Oppression through Education"* in
Black Child Journal, Summer 2017

This book is designed to partially address Dr. Hillard's call for a more comprehensive and rational planning, that will hopefully increase the efficiency and effectiveness of social justice movements, by enhancing the people. My prayer is that it will help to inspire those who are seeking a better way to fight for justice, providing them with a new perspective and a set of practical tools designed for self-refinement. We must continue to prioritize our survival and well-being, while simultaneously standing on a solid set of principles that uplift and improve our sense of integrity, empowerment, self-respect, self-worth, and the values necessary for our liberation: mind, body, and spirit. Without this, we will forever be the proverbial hamster running on the wheel, growing tired, and getting no where fast.

---

71   Work done in a non-generalizable manner, and is therefore only applicable to the question at hand, and is of limited use.

Index

Symbols

A

Ancestors 51, 61, 79, 151
Ancestral Voices 2 61
ancient 22, 25, 27, 77, 97, 133, 171, 177, 188
Angels 61, 151
Animaniacs 156
Ankh 51
ankh-right 51
anti-smoking 16
anxiety 17, 123, 124
anxious 18
APA. *See* American Psychiatric Association
archetypes 96, 97
A.S.K. Model 69
Association of Black Psychologists 34, 35, 36
Atlanta 102
attorneys 15, 17, 131
Ausar 133, 157, 180, 183
Ausar Auset Society 133, 180
Auset 97, 133, 176, 180
automatic 54, 77, 101, 129
autonomic nervous system 119, 127
autonomy 26, 155, 165
Autonomy vs. Shame and Doubt 165
awakeness 51, 60, 73, 75, 77, 78, 79, 81
awareness 19, 51, 53, 56, 57, 58, 60, 62, 63, 64, 65, 67, 68, 69, 71, 73, 74,
      75, 77, 78, 79, 80, 81, 94, 97, 127, 134, 145, 152, 153, 170, 178, 182

B

Ba 177
balance 138, 142, 148, 162, 171, 187
Baltimore 18, 40, 41
Baltimore Sun 40
Batman 56, 57, 155
Batman Vs. Superman 56, 57
behaviorism 52
benign neglect 49
bias 59, 73, 149
Big Boi 91
biofeedback 25, 56
Birth of a Nation 146
Black Flight 149

Index

Index

DuBois, W. E. B. 47
Duke, David 139

E

e-cigarettes 16
Economics 24, 189
economists 24
education 14, 83, 188, 190
EEG 52, 63
Ego 26, 61, 135, 137, 138, 145, 153, 154, 155, 156, 157, 158, 159, 160,
    161, 163, 165, 166, 167, 168, 177
ego defense mechanisms 26, 145, 157, 158, 160
  denial 158
  dissociation 160
  projection 147, 159
  reaction formation 145
  regression 160, 167
  repression 160
  sublimation 160
  suppression 157, 160
ego identity 165, 166, 167
Ego Integrity vs. Despair 165
Egypt 25, 78, 96, 176
Egyptian 29, 50, 77, 78, 87, 133, 157, 172, 184
Elektra Complex 165
Elephantine Island 25
Emanuel African Methodist Episcopal Church 130
emotional 18, 25, 28, 65, 70, 87, 104, 105, 113, 114, 117, 118, 119, 120,
    121, 122, 130, 131, 132, 133, 138, 139, 148, 155, 162, 177, 183,
    186, 187, 188
emotional intelligence 87, 188
emotions 18, 19, 28, 66, 68, 69, 70, 83, 99, 104, 113, 114, 117, 118, 119,
    120, 121, 122, 123, 124, 126, 127, 129, 130, 131, 132, 134, 139,
    151, 158, 179
empowerment 49, 143, 188, 190
energy 18, 28, 53, 56, 67, 68, 70, 127, 130, 135, 136, 163, 174, 178, 179,
    180, 182
enlightenment 51
enslavement 41, 43, 45, 46, 129, 146, 148, 162
Enslavement-era 162
Erikson, Erik 165, 166, 169

Index

Index

life coaches 25
Limitless 93
Little Albert 104, 106
lucid dreaming 77, 97
Lwa 176

M

Maat 50, 78, 183
macrosystems 40, 44
magician 15, 55, 57
Make America Great Again 133
Malcolm X 89, 139
Mami Wata 97
manipulate 15, 16, 17, 18, 26, 27, 28, 59, 62, 67, 73, 113, 127, 135, 142,
     174, 185
Manipulation 17
March for Our Lives 42
marketing 17, 24, 57, 153, 186
martial 75, 154, 178, 179, 183
mass incarceration 41
Matrix, The 86, 155
McCrae, Robert 170
Medical Apartheid 48
meditation 62, 74
Medusa 155
melancholy 171
memories 16, 63, 64, 120, 121, 154
Memphis Bleek 89
Men Ab 133, 134
mental clarity 18
mental disorders 23, 89
mental retardation 72
Metu Neter 177
microfacial expressions 25
Middle Ages 22
Milgram, Stanley 15
mind vi, 15, 21, 22, 26, 51, 52, 53, 58, 63, 64, 74, 75, 77, 81, 84, 113, 118,
     130, 142, 146, 151, 153, 157, 161, 164, 177, 178, 187
misdiagnosis 49
modern v, 19, 21, 22, 52, 55, 73, 144, 177, 188
modern psychology 22, 55, 73

Index

Index

Index

Index

About the Author

Dr. Menzise is a graduate of both Fisk and Howard Universities. He currently serves as an Associate Professor with the Morgan State University Institute for Urban Research. He received his Bachelor's and Master's degrees from Fisk in Psychology and Clinical Psychology, respectively. He finished up his clinical training at Howard where he majored in Clinical Psychology with a minor in Developmental Psychology. He completed his internship and externship with Progressive Life Center, an African-centered social service agency specializing in the NTU approach to psychotherapy and mental health services. In addition to earning his Ph.D. at Howard, Dr. Menzise also earned a graduate certificate in International Studies with a concentration in Political Science and Information & Culture.

Dr. Menzise has put his education to work on both a local and global scale. Internationally, he has worked with Ministries of Education in both the Caribbean and West Africa, conducting professional development workshops for teachers, administrators, families, students, and mental health staff. Locally, Menzise has taught thousands in the methods, philosophy and science of psychology, as well as various techniques and philosophies of Indigenous, non-Western populations.

He is an ordained multi-faith minister, and has been initiated into several ancient and traditional African spiritual sciences, all of which he incorporates in his daily life and coaching ventures. Additionally, Dr. Menzise is a member of St. John's Lodge, #3, Prince White Chapter #1, Holy

Royal Arch Masons, and King Solomon's Consistory, #20, all Prince Hall Affiliated (African Lodge #1 descendant), in Cincinnati, Ohio. He was voted an "Actual Fellow" of the Phylaxis Society, a premiere research and scholarly organization of Prince Hall Freemasons. He regularly contributes to the quarterly magazine, *Phylaxis*, and serves as Assistant Editor and cover designer for the same. Dr. Menzise has also recently been invited to serve on the publication committee for the *Black Child Journal*.

As a scholar, Dr. Menzise has presented a multitude of papers and workshops at conferences around the world. He is currently working on research designed to improve the cognitive performance of school-aged children using meditation and various "brain-training" tools. He teaches middle school, high school, undergraduate and graduate students, as well as community-based courses. Dr. Menzise has published six (6) books and two (2) decks of customized playing cards using African symbols. He served as Music Director and provided an original score for the *Ancestral Voices 2* documentary.

Jeff Menzise has been featured on nationally syndicated television and radio shows, including *NewsOneNow* with Roland Martin and *The Carl Nelson Show*. He has also been featured in national newspapers and magazines, and is the host of the hit radio show "Mind on the Matter."

Jeff Menzise is the past president (2017 - 2018) of The Association of Black Psychologists, Washington, DC Chapter.

Other Mind on the Matter Publications

WWW.MINDONTHEMATTER.COM